Rosary
Gems

DAILY WISDOM ON
THE HOLY ROSARY

Donald H. Calloway, MIC

Available from:
Marian Helpers Center
Stockbridge, MA 01263

Prayerline: 1-800-804-3823
Orderline: 1-800-462-7426
Websites: fathercalloway.com
marian.org

Imprimi Potest:
Very Rev. Kazimierz Chwalek, MIC
Provincial Superior
The Blessed Virgin Mary, Mother of Mercy Province
Congregation of Marian Fathers of the Immaculate Conception of the B.V.M.
March 25, 2015
Solemnity of the Annunciation of the Lord

ISBN: 978-1-59614-317-3
Cover Photo taken by Ileana E. Salazar, M.A. in San Ysidro, California
Design by Kathy Szpak
Editing and Proofreading: David Came and Chris Sparks

Acknowledgments: Marian Fathers of the Immaculate Conception;
Mr. and Mrs. Donald & LaChita Calloway; Matthew Calloway;
Ileana E. Salazar, M.A.; Teresa de Jesus Macias; Milanka Lachman, L.C.H.S.

April Image: Guercino, L'Immacolata Concezione
Pinacoteca Civica "F. Podesti" e Galleria d'
Arte Moderna
October Image: 'St Dominic receiving the Rosary from the Virgin Mary'
by © The Fitzwilliam Museum, Cambridge.

Printed in the United States of America

MARIAN PRESS
STOCKBRIDGE MA 01263

2015

Dedicated to

Matthew T. Calloway,
my brother in this life and
my brother in the next

*O most powerful and most
tender City of Refuge
[Mary]! Under whose
protection there is nothing for
the sinner to fear, nothing,
nothing at all! O Mother, you
are much more merciful than
can be said or thought!
The guilty sons of Adam are
received into your bosom,
immune from all fear and
danger of eternal death,
and they obtain the assurance
of a blessed Eternity.*

— Blessed Stanislaus Papczyński
Founder of the Marian Fathers
of the Immaculate Conception

The Church's devotion to the Blessed Virgin is intrinsic to Christian worship. The Church rightly honors the Blessed Virgin with special devotion. …

The liturgical feasts dedicated to the Mother of God and Marian prayer, such as the rosary, an "epitome of the whole Gospel," express this devotion to the Virgin Mary.

— *Catechism of the Catholic Church*, 971

The Second Vatican Council recommended use of the rosary to all the sons of the Church, not in express words but in unmistakable fashion in this phrase: "Let them value highly the pious practices and exercises directed to the Blessed Virgin and approved over the centuries by the Magisterium."

— Blessed Pope Paul VI, *Christi Matri*, 9

I love the rosary! Ever since my conversion to Catholicism, there has rarely been a day that has gone by that these blessed beads have not passed through my fingers. I have prayed it in church, in the mountains, in the car, on planes, alone, with others, and even while waiting for waves when surfing. I can honestly say that I do not believe I would be the man I am today without this daily companion, for there is no doubt in my mind that the rosary of Our Lady helped me discern my priestly vocation. And the rosary continues to be for me both a sure safeguard of my vow of chastity and a firm protector of my priesthood. I want to live and die with the rosary in my hands! My great love for the rosary is the reason for this book. I want others to discover the beauty, power, and wisdom of Our Lady's rosary.

You may already be aware of some of the great champions of the rosary; for example, heroic and holy men like St. Dominic, St. Louis de Montfort, and St. John Paul II. But are you aware that there are so many others who have also loved, promoted, and prayed the rosary as part of their daily path to holiness? Would you like to know something about their love for the rosary?

How about if there were a book that contained an up-to-date collection of the wisdom of these saints and popes regarding the treasure of the holy rosary! That would be a great book, don't you think? Well, the book you now have in your hands is just that book! It has taken me a long time to collect all the gems in this book, and I know you are going to be so inspired by them!

Let me note, though, that this book is not a history book on the rosary. There have been many books written on the origin, history, and spirituality of the rosary already. Rather, this book is intended as a daily devotional to help you come to a greater appreciation of the rosary by offering a daily rosary gem from some of the incredible saints and popes who have prayed it.

Yet, I don't want to presume that everyone who picks up this book is already familiar with the rosary. So, I've provided a diagram of "How to Pray the Rosary" at the end of the book (see page 211). And if you are wondering what makes the rosary so special and why it has played a major role in the lives of so many saintly Christians, the following words and wisdom of the Servant of God Frank Duff, the founder of the Legion of Mary, may offer some insight into its importance:

The rosary was established about the year 1200, and it took from the first minute. It was proposed to people, and they were encouraged to use it. It proved itself to have an affinity for the people. Ever since, it has been intertwined with Catholic life. It has been prominent in devotional literature; an element in the lives of the holy ones of the Church; the subject of the teachings of the Popes and the Doctors. The rosary has been carried by Our Lady in many of the accepted apparitions. It has entered into many of the recorded miraculous events, some of which have saved the world. It is believed to have been responsible for innumerable favors. I wonder has there been any saint since the 13th century who did not use it?

I think it is safe to say that the impact of the rosary has been huge in the life of the Church and the world. Like Frank Duff mentioned, I, too, wonder if there has been a saint since the 13th century who has not prayed it! The impact and influence of the rosary has simply been tremendous. For example, it is well known that the rosary has been the cord of strength for many marriages, as well as the lifeline that has been thrown to many lost and sinful souls, bringing them back from the brink of hell itself. It has helped countless people return to the Sacraments, been zealously used as a catechetical tool for defeating heresy, an unbreakable chain beating off temptations against chastity, a weapon that has won — or even prevented — wars, and the instrument through which many men and women have become virtuous and saintly. Only in heaven will we truly know what the rosary has done for the world and souls!

So, are you ready to discover what saintly souls have written about this most holy prayer?

Well, allow me to introduce you to a few of the amazing figures I have discovered — and whom you will read about in this book — so that you can get a hint of the power of the rosary and a foretaste of the rosary gems that are in store for you in these pages.

Have you ever heard of Blessed Bartolo Longo? I have to confess I had no idea who he was until I read St. John Paul II's letter on the Rosary (*Rosarium Virginis Mariae*). When I read that letter, I was intrigued that St. John Paul II kept mentioning a man named Blessed Bartolo Longo and how much he promoted the rosary. That piqued my interest, so I did a little research and was amazed to find out that Blessed Bartolo Longo had once been a Satanic priest! Yes, you read that right! Yet, it was through the power of the rosary that he had a radical conversion, renounced his former ways, and began to promote the rosary with zealous fervor. He became so zealous in promoting the rosary that he founded the Shrine of

Our Lady of the Rosary in Pompeii, Italy, and became known as the "Apostle of the Rosary" for the 19th century. I have amazing rosary gems from him in this book for you!

Or what about Blessed Ceferino Giménez Malla? Again, I confess that I did not know about this great man either until one day I read about a newly beatified man whom the Pope classified a "Martyr of the Rosary." As it turns out, Blessed Ceferino was a gypsy from Spain and loved the rosary so much that at one point during the Spanish Civil war (1936-1939), he was arrested by secular authorities and instructed to surrender his rosary beads or risk being shot. That wasn't going to happen, though, not for this champion of the rosary. Blessed Ceferino, in heroic saintly fashion, preferred to be shot and die with the rosary in his hands rather than give up his rosary! Wait till you read what both St. John Paul II and Pope Benedict XVI said about him!

How about Pope Leo XIII? Know much about him? He was pope from 1878 to 1903, and was the oldest living pope we have ever had, holding that office until his death at the age of 93! Not only was he the oldest and longest-living pope we have ever had, but he also wrote no less than 11 encyclicals and five apostolic letters on the rosary! Wow! No other pope has even come close to writing that many official documents on the rosary. For this reason he is called the "Rosary Pope." You will discover many gems from his encyclicals and apostolic letters in this book. They are profound and so apropos for our times.

Then there's the saint known as "Father Hail Mary." Who is that? Well, his name is St. Simón de Rojas. He was a Trinitarian priest who served the poor in Spain and founded the Congregation of the Slaves of Mary. He lived from 1552-1624. Saint Simón was so devoted to the rosary that he would ship large packages of hand-made rosaries to England in order to evangelize those who were falling away from the one true Church during the turbulent times of the Protestant revolt. He gained the title "Father Hail Mary" because he recited the *Ave Maria* prayer so frequently that people began to refer to him as the "Apostle of the *Ave Maria*," or "Father Hail Mary." Is that awesome or what?

What about Blesseds Luigi and Maria Beltrame Quattrocchi? Ever heard of them? What an incredible couple they were. They were the first married couple to be beatified together. When they were beatified together in 2001, a number of their children were still living and present for the ceremony! And guess what helped to make this extraordinary couple so holy and worthy of beatification? Yep, you guessed it: the daily rosary. As a couple, they would pray it every evening before going to bed, and they were married for 45 years! That's a lot of rosaries!

And, of course, there is the indefatigable Servant of God Father Patrick Peyton. This Irish-American priest was known the world over as the "Rosary Priest" and miraculously gathered together the most famous Hollywood celebrities of the mid-20th century in order to have them pray the rosary on national and international television and radio programs. Fr. Peyton loved the rosary of Our Lady so much that he became unparalleled in his zeal and desire to bring the holy rosary to the entire world, especially families. He would literally travel all over the globe gathering crowds of hundreds of thousands of people (sometimes even millions of people) to pray the rosary!

And the list goes on and on! For me personally, discovering such zealous lovers of the rosary makes me want to renew and increase my love for the rosary, and experience a new fervor in praying it!

You will find much inspiration in this book for renewing your love for the rosary, too. For example, Blessed James Alberione, a saintly priest who sought to evangelize through using modern means of communication, once noted the following:

> The rosary is an easy devotion. It is composed of prayers which everyone learns as a child — prayers which can be said without any effort or difficulty. The rosary can be recited at any time, in any place and in any circumstance.

The rosary is pleasing to the Blessed Virgin because of its origin and its excellence. In fact, the rosary is not the product of human fancy; it was suggested to men by the Blessed Virgin herself, and she had the most sublime purpose for doing so. Mary personally gave us this precious token of salvation, and she also taught us the manner of using it. Is there any devotion [to Mary] more excellent than this?

This is why I put this book together and offer it to you. The more we realize that the rosary has power, is easy to pray, and is most pleasing to heaven, and the more witnesses that verify this, the more we are encouraged to take up this Marian treasure with new fervor. Our times need the rosary more than ever! Saint John Paul II once even noted the following:

The history of the rosary shows how this prayer was used in particular by the Dominicans at a difficult time for the Church due to the spread of heresy. Today we are facing new challenges. Why should we not once more have recourse to the rosary, with the same faith as those who have gone before us?

Yes! That's it! Following the wisdom of the saints and popes, let's take up the rosary with renewed fervor and help bring back a culture of life, love, and light.

Lastly, so that heaven and earth are united in the pages you are about to read, and as an additional aid to prayer, you will find that after each rosary gem, I have added an invocation to a saint or a blessed. For the most part, I have selected saints and blesseds who have lived since the 13th century and who most likely prayed the rosary themselves.

Let's pray the rosary!

Fr. Donald Calloway, MIC, STL
Vicar Provincial
The Blessed Virgin Mary, Mother of Mercy Province

JANUARY

January 1

The holy rosary introduces us into the very heart of faith. With our thought fixed on it, we greet repeatedly, joyfully, the holy Mother of God; declare blessed the Son, the sweet fruit of her womb; and invoke her motherly protection in life and in death.

– St. John Paul II

Mary, Mother of God, pray for us!

January 2

It is mainly to expand the Kingdom of Christ that we look to the rosary for the most effective help.

– Pope Leo XIII

Blessed Marie-Anne Vaillot, pray for us!

January 3

I could conquer the world if I had
an army to say the rosary.

— BLESSED POPE PIUS IX

St. Elizabeth Ann Seton, pray for us!

January 4

The beauty of the rosary is that it is not merely a vocal
prayer. It is also a mental prayer. One sometimes hears a
dramatic presentation in which, while the human voice
is speaking, there is a background of beautiful music,
giving force and dignity to the words.
The rosary is like that.

— VENERABLE FULTON J. SHEEN

Blessed Manuel González García, pray for us!

January 5

The holy rosary is to me the most
beautiful of all devotions.

– ST. JOHN NEUMANN

St. John Neumann, pray for us!

January 6

In climbing toward God for its salvation,
the soul possesses the Key of Heaven in the rosary.

– SERVANT OF GOD
(FR.) DOLINDO RUOTOLO

St. André Bessette, pray for us!

January 7

The rosary is not *a* devotion to
the Blessed Virgin; it is *the* devotion to Mary!

– VENERABLE PAULINE MARIE JARICOT

Blessed Edward Waterson, pray for us!

January 8

From my earliest memories,
I saw my father with the rosary beads in
his hands and my mother holding hers.

– SERVANT OF GOD
(FR.) PATRICK PEYTON

Blessed Gabriele Allegra, pray for us!

January 9

The rosary, a simple and easy prayer,
helps me to be a child.

– SERVANT OF GOD POPE JOHN PAUL I

Blessed Tommaso Reggio, pray for us!

January 10

Even if you have to fight distractions all through your
whole rosary, be sure to fight well, arms in hand: that
is to say, do not stop saying your rosary even if it is
hard to say and you have absolutely no sensible
devotion. It is a terrible battle, I know, but one
that is profitable to the faithful soul.

– ST. LOUIS DE MONTFORT

Blessed Anna of the Angels Monteagudo, pray for us!

January 11

If we have spent so large a share of our activities in promoting the rosary devotion, we can easily see with what benevolence the Queen of Heaven has come to our aid when we prayed to her.

– POPE LEO XIII

Blessed William Carter, pray for us!

January 12

There is no devotion so generally practiced by the faithful of all classes as that of the rosary.

– ST. ALPHONSUS LIGUORI

St. Marguerite Bourgeoys, pray for us!

January 13

Amid the disharmony of our chaotic lives,
the rosary is the instrument, the harp or the psaltery
with its ten chords, for each group of harmonies.
With the rosary, we continually raise a
song of love from the earth.

– SERVANT OF GOD (FR.) DOLINDO RUOTOLO

St. Marianne Cope, pray for us!

January 14

I do not know how this should be, but it is perfectly
true; and I know no surer way of discovering whether
a person belongs to God than by finding out if he
loves saying the Hail Mary and the rosary.

– ST. LOUIS DE MONTFORT

Blessed Peter Donders, pray for us!

January 15

The rosary is a Gospel prayer.

– BLESSED POPE PAUL VI

St. Francisco Fernández de Capillas, pray for us!

January 16

[Saint] Joseph Vaz was on fire with faith. Guided by
the example of his Divine Master, he travelled the
whole island [of Sri Lanka], going everywhere,
often barefoot, with a rosary round his neck
as a sign of his Catholic faith.

– ST. JOHN PAUL II

St. Joseph Vaz, pray for us!

January 17

I beg of you to beware of thinking of the rosary as
something of little importance — as do ignorant
people and even several great but proud scholars.
Far from being insignificant, the rosary is a priceless
treasure which is inspired by God.

– St. Louis de Montfort

Blessed Gregory Khomyshyn, pray for us!

January 18

The rosary, though clearly Marian in character,
is at heart a Christocentric prayer.

– St. John Paul II

Blessed Monique Pichery, pray for us!

January 19

The great remedy of modern times, which will
influence the events of the world more than
all diplomatic endeavors and which has
a greater effect on public life than all
organizational ones, is the rosary.

– SERVANT OF GOD
(FR.) JOSEPH KENTENICH

St. Tommaso of Cori, pray for us!

January 20

The rosary can bring families through
all dangers and evils.

– SERVANT OF GOD
(FR.) PATRICK PEYTON

Blessed Cyprian Michael Iwene Tansi, pray for us!

January 21

It is well known that there have been many persons
occupied in most weighty functions or absorbed in
laborious cares who have never omitted for a single day
this pious practice [the rosary]. Combined with this
advantage is that inward sentiment of devotion which
attracts minds to the rosary, so that they love it as the
intimate companion and faithful protector of life.

– POPE LEO XIII

Blessed Edward Stransham, pray for us!

January 22

How could one possibly contemplate the mystery of
the Child in Bethlehem, in the joyful mysteries
[of the rosary], without experiencing the desire to
welcome, defend, and promote life, and to shoulder
the burdens of suffering children all over the world?

– ST. JOHN PAUL II

St. Gianna Beretta Molla, pray for us!

January 23

The rosary is like a crown of roses, like a diadem with which the faithful adorn the head of their Queen, hoping, quite rightly, that the Blessed Virgin Mary will prevail against their enemies.

– BLESSED WILLIAM JOSEPH CHAMINADE

Blessed William Joseph Chaminade, pray for us!

January 24

The example of St. Francis de Sales, the great spiritual director of his time, should spur you on to join the holy confraternity of the rosary, since, great saint that he was, he bound himself by oath to say the whole rosary every single day as long as he lived.

– ST. LOUIS DE MONTFORT

St. Francis de Sales, pray for us!

January 25

With the rosary, the Christian people
sits at the school of Mary.

– St. John Paul II

St. Donald of Ogilvy, pray for us!

January 26

If you say the holy rosary every day,
with a spirit of faith and love, Our Lady
will make sure she leads you very
far along her Son's path.

– St. Josemaría Escrivá

Blessed Michal Kozal, pray for us

January 27

Every Our Father and Hail Mary [of the rosary],
like bread from heaven, reinforces our strength.

– BLESSED GEORGE MATULAITIS

Blessed George Matulaitis, pray for us!

January 28

From her [Mary], St. Thomas Aquinas sought
celestial wisdom daily with the holy rosary.

– BLESSED JAMES ALBERIONE

St. Thomas Aquinas, pray for us

January 29

If you wish to convert anyone to the fullness of the knowledge
of our Lord and of his Mystical Body, then teach him the
rosary. One of two things will happen. Either he will stop
saying the rosary — or he will get the gift of faith.

– VENERABLE FULTON J. SHEEN

Blessed Boleslava Lament, pray for us!

January 30

It has always been common knowledge that those who bear the sign of reprobation, such as all formal heretics, evil-doers, the proud, and the worldly, hate and spurn the Hail Mary and the rosary. True, heretics learn to say the Our Father but they will not countenance the Hail Mary and the rosary, and they would rather carry a snake around with them than a rosary.

– St. Louis de Montfort

St. Mutien-Marie Wiaux, pray for us!

January 31

The snake is a symbol of the devil, whereas the rope stands for *Ave Maria*, or rather the rosary, a succession of Hail Marys with which we can strike, conquer, and destroy all of Hell's demons.

– St. John Bosco

St. John Bosco, pray for us!

FEBRUARY

February 1

Experience has shown that to inculcate love for the
Mother of God deeply in souls there is nothing more
efficacious than the practice of the rosary. We exhort
all the faithful to practice this devotion.

– POPE LEO XIII

Blessed Marie Cassin, pray for us!

February 2

How often on meditating on the mysteries of the rosary,
when this mystery comes up [Presentation of the Lord in
the Temple], I have wept in sorrow and in love.

– VENERABLE CONCEPCIÓN CABRERA DE ARMIDA

St. Jeanne de Lestonnac, pray for us!

February 3

In the rosary,
we not only *say* prayers;
we *think* them.

– VENERABLE FULTON J. SHEEN

Blessed Anne-Marie Rivier, pray for us!

February 4

From my youthful years, this prayer
[the rosary] has held an important
place in my spiritual life.

– ST. JOHN PAUL II

St. Joan of Valois, pray for us!

February 5

Happy are those who recite the holy rosary
with understanding. They will learn all that is
of faith, light, hope, and love in it.

– St. Clement Hofbauer

Blessed Elizabeth Canori Mora, pray for us!

February 6

Her [Blessed Rosalie Rendu's] charity was inventive.
Where did she draw the strength to carry out so many
things? From her intense prayer life and the continuous
praying of the rosary, which she never abandoned.

– St. John Paul II

Blessed Rosalie Rendu, pray for us!

February 7

Among all the devotions approved by the Church,
none has been so favored by so many
miracles as the rosary devotion.

– BLESSED POPE PIUS IX

Blessed Pope Pius IX, pray for us!

February 8

I want to get ten million families
to pray the rosary every day.

– SERVANT OF GOD (FR.) PATRICK PEYTON

St. Josephine Bakhita, pray for us!

February 9

The rosary represents a symbol of Mary's graces. Christians invoke her as "Queen of the most holy rosary," which conjures up the brilliant conquests of faith over evil and over religious ignorance.

– POPE LEO XIII

Blessed Anne Catherine Emmerich, pray for us!

February 10

The rosary is the book of the blind, where souls see and there enact the greatest drama of love the world has ever known; it is the book of the simple, which initiates them into mysteries and knowledge more satisfying than the education of other men; it is the book of the aged, whose eyes close upon the shadow of this world and open on the substance of the next.

– VENERABLE FULTON J. SHEEN

Blessed José Sánchez del Río, pray for us!

February 11

Without thinking what I was doing, I took my
rosary in my hands and went to my knees.
The Lady made a sign of approval with
her head and took into her hands her own
rosary which hung from her right arm.

– ST. BERNADETTE SOUBIROUS

Our Lady of Lourdes, pray for us!

February 12

At Lourdes, the Immaculata used the beads
of the rosary, and thereby encouraged
Bernadette to recite it.

– ST. MAXIMILIAN KOLBE

Blessed María Dolores Rodríguez Sopeña, pray for us!

February 13

In Mary, God has given us the most zealous
guardian of Christian unity. There are, of course,
more ways than one to win her protection by
prayer, but as for us, we think that the best and
most effective way to her favor lies in the rosary.

– POPE LEO XIII

St. Catherine de Ricci, pray for us!

February 14

Because of the daily family rosary, my home
was for me a cradle, a school, a university,
a library, and most of all, a little church.

– SERVANT OF GOD (FR.) PATRICK PEYTON

Blessed Vicente Vilar David, pray for us!

February 15

Of all our prayers to the Mother of Mercy, the one
which the Church urges us most insistently [to pray]
is the rosary, the recital of which God rewards
with countless graces and blessings.

– BLESSED MICHAEL SOPOCKO

Blessed Michael Sopocko, pray for us!

February 16

Love the Madonna and pray the rosary,
for her rosary is the weapon against
the evils of the world today.

– ST. PADRE PIO

Blessed Giuseppe Allamano, pray for us!

February 17

Devotion to Our Lady of the Rosary in its doctrinal foundations is as old as the Church.

– SERVANT OF GOD (FR.) JOHN HARDON

St. Alexis Falconieri, pray for us!

February 18

Almighty God has given it [the rosary] to you because he wants you to use it as a means to convert the most hardened sinners and the most obstinate heretics. He has attached to it grace in this life and glory in the next.

– ST. LOUIS DE MONTFORT

St. Geltrude Comensoli, pray for us!

February 19

I'll say as many rosaries as you want!

– BLESSED FRANCISCO MARTO

Blessed Francisco Marto, pray for us!

February 20

At the end of the rosary,
she [Blessed Jacinta Marto] always said
three Hail Marys for the Holy Father.

– SERVANT OF GOD LÚCIA DOS SANTOS

Blessed Jacinta Marto, pray for us!

February 21

It is the rosary prayed by families that will
keep the lights of faith glowing in the days of
darkness of faith, as it has done in the past.

– SERVANT OF GOD (FR.) PATRICK PEYTON

St. Peter Damian, pray for us!

February 22

She [Mary] prays with us. The rosary prayer
embraces the problems of the Church, of the See of
St. Peter, and the problems of the whole world.

– ST. JOHN PAUL II

Blessed Stefan Wincenty Frelichowski, pray for us!

February 23

The rosary is the most excellent form of
prayer and the most efficacious means of
attaining eternal life. It is the remedy for all
our evils, the root of all our blessings. There
is no more excellent way of praying.

– POPE LEO XIII

Blessed Josephine Vannini, pray for us!

February 24

To recite the rosary is nothing
other than to contemplate
with Mary the face of Christ.

– ST. JOHN PAUL II

Blessed Tommaso Maria Fusco, pray for us!

February 25

Gentle in manner and determined in her commitment, she [Blessed María Ludovica de Angelis] always had the rosary in her hands.

– St. John Paul II

Blessed María Ludovica de Angelis, pray for us!

February 26

When very frequently we receive newly married couples in audience and address paternal words to them, we give them rosaries, we recommend these to them earnestly, and we exhort them, citing our own example, not to let even one day pass without saying the rosary, no matter how burdened they may be with many cares and labors.

– Pope Pius XI

Blessed Jacques-Désiré Laval, pray for us!

February 27

Today, as in other times, the rosary must be a powerful weapon to enable us to win in our interior struggle, and to help all souls.

– St. Josemaría Escrivá

Blessed Maria Caridad Brader, pray for us!

February 28

When the Holy Spirit has revealed this secret [of the rosary] to a priest and director of souls, how blessed is that priest! If a priest really understands this secret, he will say the rosary every day and will encourage others to say it.

– St. Louis de Montfort

Blessed Villana de'Botti, pray for us!

February 29

When parents and children gather together at the end
of the day in the recitation of the rosary, together they
meditate on the example of work, obedience, and
charity which shone in the house of Nazareth; together
they learn from the Mother of God to suffer serenely;
to accept with dignity and courage the difficulties of life,
and to acquire the proper attitude to the daily events of
life. It is certain that they will meet with greater facility
the problems of family life. Homes will thereby be
converted into sanctuaries of peace. Torrents of divine
favors will come to them, even the inestimable
favor of a priestly or religious vocation.

– ST. POPE JOHN XXIII

St. Philomena, pray for us!

MARCH

March 1

Countless families the world over invite Mary to their
home through the family rosary. She comes.
They sense her presence. They solve their
problems because where Mary is present
there is Christ, her Divine Son.

– SERVANT OF GOD (FR.) PATRICK PEYTON

Blessed José Gabriel del Rosario Brochero, pray for us!

March 2

If you desire peace in your hearts,
in your homes, in your country, assemble
every evening to recite the rosary.

– BLESSED POPE PIUS IX

St. Angela of the Cross, pray for us!

March 3

Concentration is impossible when the mind is troubled; thoughts run helter-skelter; a thousand and one images flood across the mind; distracted and wayward, the spiritual seems a long way off. The rosary is the best therapy for these distraught, unhappy, fearful, and frustrated souls, precisely because it involves the simultaneous use of three powers: the physical, the vocal, and the spiritual, and in that order.

– VENERABLE FULTON J. SHEEN

St. Katherine Drexel, pray for us!

March 4

It [the rosary] shows, through the vicissitudes of the Son of God and of the Virgin, how constant in human life is the alteration of good and evil, calm and storms, joyful days and sad ones.

– ST. JOHN PAUL II

Blessed Matthias Araki, pray for us!

March 5

The holy rosary is a powerful weapon.
Use it with confidence, and you'll be
amazed at the results.

— St. Josemaría Escrivá

Blessed Dionysius Fugishima, pray for us!

March 6

For every time we devoutly say the rosary in
supplication before her, we are once more brought
face to face with the marvel of our salvation; we
watch the mysteries of our Redemption as though
they were unfolding before our eyes; and as one
follows another, Mary stands revealed at
once as God's Mother and our Mother.

— Pope Leo XIII

St. Atilano Cruz Alvarado, pray for us!

March 7

The rosary, reclaimed in its full meaning,
goes to the heart of Christian life.

– St. John Paul II

Blessed John Larke, pray for us!

March 8

All the idle moments of one's life can be sanctified, thanks to the
rosary. As we walk the streets, we pray with the rosary hidden
in our hand or in our pocket; as we are driving an automobile,
the little knobs under most steering wheels can serve as counters
for the decades. While waiting to be served at a lunchroom,
or waiting for a train, or in a store, or while playing dummy
at bridge, or when conversation or a lecture lags —
all these moments can be sanctified and made to serve
inner peace, thanks to a prayer that enables one
to pray at all times and under all circumstances.

– Venerable Fulton J. Sheen

St. Siméon François Berneux, pray for us!

March 9

By its nature, the recitation of the rosary calls for
a quiet rhythm and a lingering pace, helping the
individual to meditate on the mysteries of the
Lord's life as seen through the eyes of
her who was closest to the Lord.

– BLESSED POPE PAUL VI

St. Dominic Savio, pray for us!

March 10

The *Angelus* prayer, like the rosary, should be for
every Christian, and even more for Christian families,
a spiritual oasis in the course of the day,
to find courage and confidence.

– ST. JOHN PAUL II

St. John Ogilvie, pray for us!

March 11

The rosary has very great riches, both in the Hail Mary and in the mysteries contemplated. It is not a monotonous mumbling. It is a marvelous harmony, just as a musical instrument does not play a dull repetition of a note, but a melodic and harmonious variation, which raises the soul and arouses in it much affection and sweet and pure thoughts. It is almost a vibration of waves and the delicacy of musical chords.

– SERVANT OF GOD (FR.) DOLINDO RUOTOLO

St. Mateo Correa, pray for us!

March 12

What a blessed thing it would be if we could pray the rosary over nationwide radio and bring Our Blessed Mother into every home in America.

– SERVANT OF GOD (FR.) PATRICK PEYTON

St. Luigi Orione, pray for us!

March 13

There is no surer means of calling down God's
blessings upon the family and especially of
preserving happiness in the home than
the daily recitation of the rosary.

– VENERABLE POPE PIUS XII

Blessed Bedřich Bachstein, pray for us!

March 14

Individuals, whatever their spiritual status may be, will
undoubtedly find in the fervent recitation of the holy
rosary an invitation to regulate their lives in conformity
with Christian principles. They will, in truth, find in
the rosary a spring of most abundant graces to help
them in fulfilling faithfully their duties in life.

– ST. POPE JOHN XXIII

Blessed Giacomo Cusmano, pray for us!

March 15

When parents pray the rosary, at the end of
each decade, they should hold the rosary aloft
and say to her [Mary], "With these beads
bind my children to your Immaculate Heart,"
and she will attend to their souls.

– ST. LOUISE DE MARILLAC

St. Louise de Marillac, pray for us!

March 16

One thing that makes me strong every day is praying
the rosary to Our Lady. I feel such great strength
because I go to her and I feel strong.

– POPE FRANCIS

Blessed John Amias, pray for us!

March 17

The succession of Hail Marys [of the rosary]
constitutes the warp on which is woven the
contemplation of the mysteries.

– BLESSED POPE PAUL VI

St. John Sarkander, pray for us!

March 18

If properly revitalized, the rosary is an aid and
certainly not a hindrance to ecumenism!

– ST. JOHN PAUL II

St. Richard Pampuri, pray for us!

March 19

Let all men, the learned and the ignorant,
the just and the sinners, the great and the small,
praise and honor Jesus and Mary, night and day,
by saying the most holy rosary.

– ST. LOUIS DE MONTFORT

St. Joseph, pray for us

March 20

Saint Jozef Bilczewski was a man of prayer.
The Holy Mass, the Liturgy of the Hours,
meditation, the rosary, and other pious
practices formed part of his daily life.

– POPE BENEDICT XVI

St. Jozef Bilczewski, pray for us!

March 21

As an army has its march music, marking the time
for the soldiers, so does the rosary lovingly
mark time for the Church Militant.

– SERVANT OF GOD (FR.) DOLINDO RUOTOLO

Blessed Maria Candida of the Eucharist, pray for us!

March 22

To say the holy rosary, considering the mysteries,
repeating the Our Father and Hail Mary, with the
praises to the Blessed Trinity, and the constant
invocation of the Mother of God, is a continuous act
of faith, hope, and love, of adoration and reparation.

– ST. JOSEMARÍA ESCRIVÁ

St. Nicholas Owen, pray for us!

March 23

My only purpose in thirty-three years of service
has been that of saving my soul and that of my
brother by spreading the most holy rosary.

— Blessed Bartolo Longo

St. Joseph Oriol, pray for us!

March 24

Meditating on the mysteries of the holy rosary,
we learn, after the example of Mary, to have peace in
our souls through the unceasing and loving contact
with Jesus and the mysteries of his redemptive life.

— Blessed Pope Paul VI

Blessed Alberto Marvelli, pray for us!

March 25

The repetition of the Hail Mary in the rosary gives us a share in God's own wonder and pleasure: in jubilant amazement, we acknowledge the greatest miracle in history.

– St. John Paul II

Blessed Omelyan Kovch, pray for us!

March 26

We must hold fast to the treasure of the rosary,
· the gift of Our Blessed Mother.

– Servant of God (Fr.) Patrick Peyton

Blessed Magdalena Caterina Morano, pray for us!

March 27

Meditation on the mysteries of the rosary, often repeated in the spirit of faith, cannot help but please her [Mary] and move her, the fondest of mothers, to show mercy to her children.

– Pope Leo XIII

St. Jenaro Sánchez Delgadillo, pray for us!

March 28

How could love not be made more fervent by
the rosary? We meditate on the suffering and
death of our Redeemer and the sorrows
of his afflicted Mother.

– POPE PIUS XI

Blessed Bartolomé Blanco Márquez, pray for us!

March 29

It is really pathetic to see how most people say the holy rosary
— they say it astonishingly fast and mumble so that the words
are not properly pronounced at all. We could not possibly
expect anyone, even the most unimportant person, to think
that a slipshod address of this kind was a compliment, and yet
we expect Jesus and Mary to be pleased with it!

– ST. LOUIS DE MONTFORT

Blessed Jerzy Popieluszko, pray for us!

March 30

The rosary belongs among the finest and most praiseworthy traditions of Christian contemplation.

– St. John Paul II

St. Leonard Murialdo, pray for us!

March 31

If you say the rosary faithfully until death, I do assure you that, in spite of the gravity of your sins, you shall receive a never-fading crown of glory. Even if you are on the brink of damnation, even if you have one foot in hell, even if you have sold your soul to the devil as sorcerers do who practice black magic, and even if you are a heretic as obstinate as a devil, sooner or later you will be converted and will amend your life and save your soul, if — and mark well what I say — if you say the holy rosary devoutly every day until death for the purpose of knowing the truth and obtaining contrition and pardon for your sins.

– St. Louis de Montfort

St. Román Adame Rosales, pray for us!

APRIL

April 1

Windhorst, a German, was invited one time by certain friends not practicing the Faith to show them his beads; it was a joke; they had previously taken them from his left pocket. Windhorst, not having found them in his left pocket, put his hand in his right pocket and came out the victor. He always had an extra rosary.

– SERVANT OF GOD POPE JOHN PAUL I

Blessed Anacleto González Flores, pray for us!

April 2

The rosary is by far the best prayer by which to plead before her [Mary] the cause of our separated brethren.

– POPE LEO XIII

St. Pedro Calungsod, pray for us!

April 3

Airplanes must have runways before they can fly.
What the runway is to the airplane, that the rosary
beads are to prayer — the physical start
to gain spiritual altitude.

– VENERABLE FULTON J. SHEEN

St. Hermann Joseph, pray for us!

April 4

The well-meditated rosary consists in a threefold
element. For each decade, there is a picture, and
for each picture, a threefold emphasis, which
is simultaneously, mystical contemplation,
intimate reflection, and pious intention.

– ST. POPE JOHN XXIII

St. Gaetano Catanoso, pray for us!

April 5

Saint Vincent Ferrer said to a man who was dying in despair, "Why are you determined to lose your soul when Jesus Christ wishes to save you?" The man answered that, in spite of Christ, he was determined to go to hell. The Saint replied, "And you, in spite of yourself, shall be saved." He [St. Vincent] began with the persons in the house to recite the rosary; when, behold, the sick man asked to make his confession; and having done so with many tears, expired.

– St. Alphonsus Liguori

St. Vincent Ferrer, pray for us!

April 6

We must never forget the rosary and its meaning, the very embodiment of our Christianity.

– Servant of God (Fr.) Patrick Peyton

Blessed Pierina Morosini, pray for us!

April 7

Since the holy rosary is composed, principally and in substance, of the Prayer of Christ and the Angelic Salutation, that is, the Our Father and the Hail Mary, it was without doubt the first prayer and the first devotion of the faithful and has been in use all through the centuries, from the time of the apostles and disciples down to the present.

– ST. LOUIS DE MONTFORT

Blessed Domingo Iturrate Zubero, pray for us!

April 8

The revival of the rosary in Christian families, within the context of a broader pastoral ministry to the family, will be an effective aid to countering the devastating effects of the crises typical of our age.

– ST. JOHN PAUL II

St. Julia Billiart, pray for us!

April 9

The rosary is a teacher of life, a teacher full of
gentleness and love, where people beneath the gaze
of Mary, almost without noticing, discover they are
being slowly educated in preparation for the second
life, that which is authentic life, for it is not destined
to end in a very few years, but to go unto eternity.

– BLESSED BARTOLO LONGO

St. Euphrasia Eluvathingal, pray for us!

April 10

The rosary is an exercise of piety
that draws its motivating force from the
liturgy and leads naturally back to it.

– BLESSED POPE PAUL VI

Blessed Anthony Neyrot, pray for us!

April 11

It could be said that each mystery of the rosary,
carefully meditated, sheds light on
the mystery of man.

– ST. JOHN PAUL II

St. Gemma Galgani, pray for us!

April 12

I am convinced that the mere distribution of alms
and pious books will produce no fruit unless it is
accompanied by prayer. Among the treasures the
Church has collected, the rosary seems to us
to respond best to our needs.

– VENERABLE PAULINE JARICOT

St. Agustín Caloca Cortés, pray for us!

April 13

The rosary should be said with devotion.

– St. Alphonsus Liguori

St. Pope Martin I, pray for us!

April 14

The holy rosary drives away family disintegration and is a secure bond of communion and peace.

– St. John Paul II

St. Peter González, pray for us!

April 15

The rosary is a school of prayer;
the rosary is a school of faith!

– POPE FRANCIS

Blessed Maria Troncatti, pray for us!

April 16

When people say the rosary together, it is far more
formidable to the devil than one said privately,
because in this public prayer, it is an army that is
attacking him. He can often overcome the prayer
of an individual, but if this prayer is joined to that
of other Christians, the devil has much more
trouble in getting the best of it. It is very easy
to break a single stick, but if you join it to others
to make a bundle, it cannot be broken.

– ST. LOUIS DE MONTFORT

St. Bernadette Soubirous, pray for us!

April 17

It would be impossible to name all the many
saints who discovered in the rosary a
genuine path to growth in holiness.

– St. JOHN PAUL II

St. Benedict Joseph Labre, pray for us!

April 18

Our Lady has shown her thorough approval of
the name rosary; she has revealed to several
people that each time they say a Hail Mary they
are giving her a beautiful rose and that each
complete rosary makes her a crown of roses.

– St. LOUIS DE MONTFORT

Blessed Marie-Anne Blondin, pray for us

April 19

The rosary is a powerful prayer against Satan and against
the assaults of evil. Our Church brought, and continues to
bring, great triumphs because of this prayer. The decades
of the rosary, from this point of view, are like the belt of
a machine gun: every bead is a shot, every affection
of the soul is as an explosion of faith that frightens
off Satan, and Mary once more crushes his head.

– SERVANT OF GOD (FR.) DOLINDO RUOTOLO

Blessed James Duckett, pray for us!

April 20

If the rosary be hurt [neglected],
Mary's place will be diminished, and so
will the quantity of prayer in our lives.

– SERVANT OF GOD FRANK DUFF

St. Agnes of Montepulciano, pray for us!

April 21

Kings and princes, burdened with most
urgent occupations and affairs, made it
their duty to recite the rosary.

– POPE PIUS XI

St. Lorenzo Ruiz, pray for us!

April 22

Just as two friends, frequently in each other's company,
tend to develop similar habits, so, too, by holding
familiar converse with Jesus and the Blessed Virgin, by
meditating on the mysteries of the rosary, and by living
the same life in Holy Communion, we can become, to
the extent of our lowliness, similar to them, and can
learn from these supreme models a life of humility,
poverty, hiddenness, patience, and perfection

– BLESSED BARTOLO LONGO

Blessed Maria Gabriella Sagheddu, pray for us!

April 23

Don't be upset. Let's say the rosary
and recall Jesus' wounds.

– Venerable María del Carmen
González-Valerio

St. Augustin Schoeffler, pray for us!

April 24

The rosary is the prayer which God,
through his Church and Our Lady,
has recommended most insistently to us all
as a road to and gateway of salvation.

– Servant of God Lúcia Dos Santos

St. Benedetto Menni, pray for us!

April 25

The special value of the rosary lies in the
special way in which it looks at the mysteries;
for with all our thoughts of him [Jesus]
are mingled thoughts of his Mother.

– BLESSED JOHN HENRY NEWMAN

Blessed Robert Anderton, pray for us!

April 26

Contemplating the scenes of the rosary in union
with Mary is a means of learning from her to
"read" Christ, to discover his secrets
and to understand his message.

– ST. JOHN PAUL II

Blessed Rolando Rivi, pray for us!

April 27

Adorned by us with garlands of her favorite prayer
[the rosary], she will obtain by her entreaties help
in abundance from the Spirit that quickeneth.

– POPE LEO XIII

St. Lawrence Huong, pray for us!

April 28

Never will anyone really be able to understand the
marvelous riches of sanctification which are contained
in the prayers and mysteries of the holy rosary. This
meditation on the mysteries of the life and death of
our Lord and Savior Jesus Christ is the source of the
most wonderful fruits for those who use it.

– ST. LOUIS DE MONTFORT

St. Louis de Montfort, pray for us!

April 29

Like all the works and events in the
Church, the rosary has the power and
touch of the Holy Spirit upon it.

– SERVANT OF GOD (FR.) PATRICK PEYTON

St. Catherine of Siena, pray for us!

April 30

Do you want to love Our Lady?
Well, then, get to know her. How?
By praying her rosary.

– ST. JOSEMARÍA ESCRIVÁ

St. Pope Pius V, pray for us!

MAY

May I

In this month of May, I would like to recall the
importance and beauty of the prayer of the holy
rosary. Reciting the Hail Mary, we are led to contemplate the mysteries of Jesus, that is, to reflect on the
key moments of his life, so that, as with Mary and St.
Joseph, he is the center of our thoughts, of our attention, and our actions. It would be nice if, especially in
this month of May, we could pray the holy rosary
together in the family, with friends, in the parish, or
some prayer to Jesus and the Virgin Mary!

– POPE FRANCIS

St. Joseph the Worker, pray for us!

May 2

During the month of May,
we used to recite the rosary
as a family every day.

– SERVANT OF GOD
LÚCIA DOS SANTOS

St. José Mariá Rubio, pray for us!

May 3

No normal mind yet has ever been
overcome by worries or fears who
was faithful to the rosary.

– VENERABLE FULTON J. SHEEN

Blessed Marie-Léonie Paradis, pray for us!

May 4

His [Blessed Ceferino Giménez Malla's] deep religious
sense was expressed in his daily participation in Holy
Mass and in the recitation of the rosary. The rosary
beads themselves, which he always kept in his pocket,
became the cause of his arrest and made Blessed
Ceferino an authentic "martyr of the rosary" because
he did not let anyone take the rosary from him,
not even when he was at the point of death.

– Pope Benedict XVI

Blessed Ceferino Giménez Malla, pray for us!

May 5

His [Blessed Ceferino Giménez Malla's] frequent participation at Mass, devotion to the Blessed Virgin with the recitation of the rosary, and his membership in various Catholic associations helped him to firmly love God and his neighbor. Thus even at the risk of his own life, he did not hesitate to defend a priest who was about to be arrested, and for doing so, he was put in prison where he never ceased to pray, and was later shot as he clutched his rosary in his hands.

– St. John Paul II

Blessed Edmund Rice, pray for us!

May 6

Do you pray the rosary every day?

– POPE FRANCIS

Blessed Anna Rosa Gattorno, pray for us!

May 7

O most holy rosary, may your flowers
bloom on the desolate flowerbeds of
unbelievers and let simple and lively
faith come to bloom again.

– SERVANT OF GOD
(FR.) DOLINDO RUOTOLO

St. Rose Venerini, pray for us!

May 8

The flowers of the
rosary never perish.

– VENERABLE POPE PIUS XII

St. Magdalene of Canossa, pray for us!

May 9

The rose is the queen of flowers,
and so the rosary is the rose of all devotions
and it is therefore the most important one.

– ST. LOUIS DE MONTFORT

Blessed Karolina Gerhardinger, pray for us!

May 10

The family that prays together stays together.
The holy rosary, by age-old tradition, has shown itself
particularly effective as a prayer which brings the
family together. Individual family members, in
turning their eyes toward Jesus, also regain the ability
to look one another in the eye, to communicate, to
show solidarity, to forgive one another and to see
their covenant of love renewed in the Spirit of God.

– St. John Paul II

St. Damien of Molokai, pray for us!

May 11

It was the Christian's faith in Mary as the Mother of
God, expressed by their ardent recitation of the
rosary, which saved Christian Europe from being
taken over by the non-Christian Muslims.

– Servant of God (Fr.) John A. Hardon

Blessed Ivan Merz, pray for us!

May 12

The history of the Church bears testimony
to the power and efficacy of this form of prayer
[the rosary], recording as it does the rout of the
Turkish forces at the naval battle of Lepanto.

– POPE LEO XIII

St. Leopold Mandić, pray for us

May 13

Say the rosary every day.

– OUR LADY OF FATIMA

Our Lady of Fatima, pray for us!

May *14*

In harmony with the tradition of many
centuries, the Lady of the message
[of Fatima] indicates the rosary, which can
rightly be defined as "Mary's prayer":
the prayer in which she feels
particularly united with us.

– St. John Paul II

St. Maria Mazzarello, pray for us!

May *15*

Among the various supplications with which
we successfully appeal to the Virgin Mother
of God, the holy rosary without doubt
occupies a special and distinct place.

– Pope Pius XI

St. Isidore, pray for us!

May 16

In the Middle Ages the Cathar sect
[Albigensian heresy] spread like wildfire.
Kings fought to destroy it.
It was overcome by the rosary.

– SERVANT OF GOD
(FR.) JOSEPH KENTENICH

St. Simon Stock, pray for us!

May 17

It is well to say the rosary kneeling before an image
of Mary, and before each decade, to make
an act of love to Jesus and Mary, and ask
them for some particular grace.

– ST. ALPHONSUS LIGUORI

Blessed Antonia Mesina, pray for us!

May 18

The rosary helps to preserve that flickering
flame of faith that has not yet been completely
extinguished from many consciences.

– SERVANT OF GOD LÚCIA DOS SANTOS

Blessed Stanislaus Papczyński, pray for us!

May 19

Starting on their wedding day, my parents knelt each
evening before the hearth to say together the family
rosary, that God and Mary might protect and bless
their home and fill it with the laughter of children.

– SERVANT OF GOD
(FR.) PATRICK PEYTON

Blessed Franz Jägerstätter, pray for us!

May 20

It would hardly be possible for me to put into
words how much Our Lady thinks of the
holy rosary and of how she vastly prefers
it to all other devotions.

– St. Louis de Montfort

St. Bernardine of Siena, pray for us!

May 21

This devotion [the rosary], so charming, needs but
little encouragement, as it is filled with happiest
thought and sweetest consolation; it must be most
dear to our Blessed Lord, as we are thinking
of him from its beginning to the end.

– Venerable Nelson Baker

St. José María Robles Hurtado, pray for us!

May 22

When I was in the fifth grade, I promised
the Virgin to pray the rosary every day.

– VENERABLE FAUSTINO PEREZ-MANGLANO

St. Rita of Cascia, pray for us!

May 23

To return to the recitation of the family rosary means
filling daily life with very different images, images of
the mystery of salvation: the image of the Redeemer,
the image of his most Blessed Mother. The family
that recites the rosary together reproduces something
of the atmosphere of the household of Nazareth:
its members place Jesus at the center.

– ST. JOHN PAUL II

St. Cristóbal Magallanes Jara, pray for us!

May 24

The rosary is a very commendable form
of prayer and meditation. In saying it we
weave a mystic garland of *Ave Marias,
Pater Nosters*, and *Gloria Patris*.

– ST. POPE JOHN XXIII

Blessed Louis-Zéphirin Moreau, pray for us!

May 25

The rosary is a very profitable kind of prayer,
provided that you understand
how to say it properly.

– ST. FRANCIS DE SALES

St. Mary Magdalene de'Pazzi, pray for us!

May 26

Saint Philip Neri walked the streets of Rome with the rosary in his hand; he sought out wayward souls and, by means of the rosary, inspired them to repent.

– BLESSED JAMES ALBERIONE

St. Philip Neri, pray for us!

May 27

We should love this exercise [the rosary], devote ourselves to it with tender piety, apply ourselves to carrying it out with the greatest attention; it is through this devotion that we will discharge the debt of love that we owe Mary.

– ST. EUGÈNE DE MAZENOD

St. Eugène de Mazenod, pray for us!

May 28

Consider the rosary as a joyful song dedicated to the Queen of Heaven, and affectionately recite it.

– ST. JOHN PAUL II

St. David Galván Bermúdez, pray for us!

May 29

Do not fail to put repeated emphasis on
the recitation of the rosary, the prayer
so pleasing to Our Lady and so often
recommended by the Roman Pontiffs.

– BLESSED POPE PAUL VI

Blessed Joseph Gérard, pray for us!

May 30

Our Lady blesses not only those who preach
her rosary, but she highly rewards all those
who get others to say it by their example.

– ST. LOUIS DE MONTFORT

St. Sabás Reyes Salazar, pray for us!

May 31

I was exhausted [after a party celebrating her birthday].
I fought hard to overcome sleep until we had said the
rosary. However, only minutes before it was to begin,
I gave in to an overpowering temptation. Hoping no
one was watching, I tiptoed to my room. In the twinkle
of an eye, I had exchanged my party dress for pajamas.
Then I knelt before my statue of Our Lady and whis-
pered, "I give you my heart and my soul, dearest
Mother Mary," and hopped into bed. As I turned to
put out the lamp on the night table, I saw Papa pass
the doorway of my room, carrying his rosary. I felt
guilty, so I called: "Papa, I have not said the rosary
today, but I am terribly sleepy." He came back to the
doorway. "*Bueno*, Princess, say a Hail Mary and go to
sleep. I'll offer the rosary for you," he said. Dear Papa
always knew how to put his princess at ease.

– Venerable Teresa of Jesus Quevedo

St. Miguel de la Mora, pray for us

JUNE

June 1

The rosary belongs among the finest
and most praiseworthy traditions
of Christian contemplation.

– St. John Paul II

Blessed Dominic of the Holy Rosary (Martyr), pray for us!

June 2

Because the rosary is both a mental and
a vocal prayer, it is one where intellectual elephants
may bathe, and the simple birds may also sip.

– Venerable Fulton J. Sheen

St. Luis Bátiz Sainz, pray for us!

June 3

As an exercise of Christian devotion among the faithful of the Latin Rite who constitute a notable portion of the Catholic family, the rosary ranks after Holy Mass and the Breviary for ecclesiastics [priests], and for the laity after participation in the Sacraments. It is a devout form of union with God and lifts souls to a high supernatural plane.

– ST. POPE JOHN XXIII

Blessed Diego Oddi, pray for us!

June 4

When we walk the streets, in whatever part of the world, the sisters [Missionaries of Charity] carry in their hands the crown of the rosary. The Virgin is our strength and our protection.

– BLESSED TERESA OF CALCUTTA

St. Filippo Smaldone, pray for us!

June 5

Every day the rosary obtains
fresh boon for Christianity.

— POPE URBAN IV

Blessed Maria Karlowska, pray for us!

June 6

Nobody can condemn devotion to the holy
rosary without condemning all that is most holy
in the Catholic Faith, such as the Lord's Prayer,
the Angelic Salutation, and the mysteries of
the life, death, and glory of Jesus Christ
and of his holy Mother.

— ST. LOUIS DE MONTFORT

St. Bonifacia Rodríguez Castro, pray for us!

June 7

The holy rosary was always,
and still is, the most acceptable devotion
to the Heart of Mother Mary.

— SERVANT OF GOD
(FR.) DOLINDO RUOTOLO

St. Anthony Mary Gianelli, pray for us!

June 8

I promise you that if you practice this devotion
and help to spread it, you will learn more from
the rosary than from any spiritual book.

— ST. LOUIS DE MONTFORT

St. Jacques Berthieu, pray for us!

June 9

To pray the rosary is to hand over our burdens to
the merciful Hearts of Christ and his Mother.

– St. John Paul II

Blessed Anna Maria Taigi, pray for us!

June 10

It remains to be added that great value and utility
accrue to the rosary from the abundance of privileges
and favors which adorn it, and more particularly from
the rich treasures of indulgences attached to it …
The Roman Pontiffs, making use of that supreme
power granted them by God, have opened out the
most abundant fountains of these graces to the
members of the sodality of the holy rosary
and to those who recite the rosary.

– Pope Leo XIII

Blessed Caspar Sadamazu, pray for us!

June 11

For a Christian, vocal prayer must spring from the heart so that, while the rosary is said, the mind can enter into contemplation of each one of the mysteries.

– St. Josemaría Escrivá

St. Paula Frassinetti, pray for us!

June 12

The rosary enlivens the hope for things above that endure forever. As we meditate on the glory of Jesus and his Mother, we see heaven opened and are heartened in our striving to gain the eternal home.

– Pope Pius XI

*Blessed Anthony Leszczewicz and
Blessed George Kaszyra, pray for us!*

June 13

The rosary is the scourge of the devil.

– POPE ADRIAN VI

St. Gaspar Bertoni, pray for us!

June 14

We like to think, and sincerely hope, that when the family gathering becomes a time of prayer, the rosary is a frequent and favored manner of praying.

– BLESSED POPE PAUL VI

Blessed Michael Tozo, pray for us!

105

June 15

By the rosary the darkness of heresy has been dispelled, and the light of the Catholic Faith shines out in all its brilliancy.

– St. Pope Pius V

Blessed Emily de Vialar, pray for us!

June 16

In an earthquake a poor woman was buried under the ruins of a house which was overthrown. A priest had the stones and rubbish cleared away, and under them found the mother with her children in her arms, alive and uninjured. On being asked what devotion she had practiced, she replied that she never omitted saying the rosary and visiting the altar of our Blessed Lady.

– St. Alphonsus Liguori

St. Jean-François Régis, pray for us!

June 17

The rosary, in a gentle, subtle way, leads one to the
Eucharist, to the Most Blessed Sacrament: those
who approach Jesus in thought, yearn to approach
him in reality; those who know Jesus cannot but
love him; indeed, those who truly love Jesus
cannot forego possessing him.

– BLESSED BARTOLO LONGO

St. Albert Chmielowski, pray for us!

June 18

A Christian who does not meditate on the
mysteries of the rosary is very ungrateful to our
Lord and shows how little he cares for all that our
Divine Savior has suffered to save the world.

– ST. LOUIS DE MONTFORT

St. Elizabeth of Schönau, pray for us!

June 19

The Hail Marys [of the rosary] transport us into
the sacred space of Mary's Heart.

– SERVANT OF GOD
(FR.) JOSEPH KENTENICH

St. Juliana Falconieri, pray for us!

June 20

Throughout history the friends of Our Blessed
Lady have devised ways and means of asking for
her power and intercession, and the most
outstanding means is the rosary.

– SERVANT OF GOD
(FR.) PATRICK PEYTON

Blessed Conor O'Devany, pray for us!

June 21

I closed my eyes and began to pray for
a while, then said a rosary.

– SERVANT OF GOD
(FR.) WALTER CISZEK

Blessed John Kinsako, pray for us!

June 22

The rosary is an easy, powerful,
and common devotion.

– BLESSED JAMES ALBERIONE

Sts. Thomas More and John Fisher, pray for us!

June 23

Abandon yourselves confidently in the hands of Mary, ceaselessly calling upon her with the rosary.

– St. John Paul II

St. Joseph Cafasso, pray for us!

June 24

If evils increase, the devotion of the People of God should also increase. And so, venerable brothers, we want you to take the lead in urging and encouraging people to pray ardently to our most merciful mother Mary by saying the rosary … this prayer is well-suited to the devotion of the People of God, most pleasing to the Mother of God and most effective in gaining heaven's blessings.

– Blessed Pope Paul VI

St. María Guadalupe García Zavala, pray for us!

June 25

The rosary is all-powerful to touch the Heart of Our Lady. It is the most excellent and fruitful type of prayer for obtaining, above all, eternal life.

– POPE LEO XIII

Blessed Paul Shinsuki, pray for us!

June 26

You always leave the rosary for later, and you end up not saying it at all because you are sleepy. If there is no other time, say it in the street without letting anybody notice it. It will, moreover, help you to have presence of God.

– ST. JOSEMARÍA ESCRIVÁ

St. Josemaría Escrivá, pray for us!

June 27

The rosary is a wonderful instrument for the
destruction of sin, the recovery of God's grace,
and the advancement of his glory.

– POPE GREGORY XII

Blessed Vasyl Velychkovsky, pray for us

June 28

To become perfect,
say a rosary a day

– ST. LOUIS DE MONTFORT

Blessed Zenon Kovalyk, pray for us!

June 29

May the rosary never fall from your hands.

– St. Pope John XXIII

Sts. Peter and Paul, pray for us!

June 30

The rosary is a sort of machine gun and atomic
bomb, namely, a weapon that is far superior to
all the weapons of modern warfare in
overcoming the enemy of God.

– Servant of God
(Fr.) Joseph Kentenich

Blessed Gennaro Sarnelli, pray for us!

JULY

July 1

[Blessed] Ignatius Falzon drew his strength
and inspiration from the Eucharist, prayer before
the Tabernacle, devotion to Mary and the rosary,
and imitation of St. Joseph.

– ST. JOHN PAUL II

Blessed Ignatius Falzon, pray for us!

July 2

The rosary is the prayer of the poor
and the rich, of the wise and the ignorant.

– SERVANT OF GOD LÚCIA DOS SANTOS

St. Junipero Serra, pray for us!

July 3

The faith of the simple can surpass that of the
learned because the intellectual often ignores those
humble means to devotion, such as medals,
pilgrimages, statues, and rosaries.

– VENERABLE FULTON J. SHEEN

Blessed Eugénie Joubert, pray for us!

July 4

If you desire peace in your hearts, in your homes,
and in your country, assemble each evening to recite
the rosary. Let not even one day pass without
saying it, no matter how burdened you may
be with many cares and labors.

– POPE PIUS XI

Blessed Pier Giorgio Frassati, pray for us!

July 5

I carry my testament [rosary]
in my pocket.

— BLESSED PIER GIORGIO FRASSATI

St. Anthony Maria Zaccaria, pray for us!

July 6

Let us pray to her [Mary] in particular with the
recitation of the holy rosary, to reach in this way,
and to help those who are laboring amid
difficulties and hardships, to make
Jesus known and loved!

— ST. JOHN PAUL II

St. Maria Goretti, pray for us!

July 7

The rosary puts all who have trust in it into communication with Our Lady.

– BLESSED POPE PAUL VI

Blessed Maria Romero Meneses, pray for us!

July 8

Never will anyone who says his rosary every day become a formal heretic or be led astray by the devil. This is a statement that I would gladly sign with my blood.

– ST. LOUIS DE MONTFORT

Blessed Nazaria Ignacia Mesa, pray for us!

July 9

The rosary is irreplaceable.

– SERVANT OF GOD FRANK DUFF

St. Veronica Giuliani, pray for us

July 10

The rosary, we are told by the Church,
is an extraordinary means of changing tepid
Christians into ardent followers of Christ.

– SERVANT OF GOD
(FR.) JOHN HARDON

Blessed Emmanuel Ruiz, pray for us!

July 11

There are certain exercises of piety which the Church recommends very much to clergy and religious. It is our wish also that the faithful, as well, should take part in these practices. The chief of these are: meditation on spiritual things, diligent examination of conscience, enclosed retreats, visits to the Blessed Sacrament, and those special prayers in honor of the Blessed Virgin Mary, among which the rosary, as all know, has pride of place.

– Venerable Pope Pius XII

St. Oliver Plunkett, pray for us!

July 12

The rosary has proven itself as a friend in the life and work of great men.

– Servant of God (Fr.) Joseph Kentenich

Blesseds Louis and Zélie Martin, pray for us!

July 13

The fathers and mothers of families particularly must give an example to their children, especially when, at sunset, they gather together after the day's work, within the domestic walls and recite the holy rosary on bended knees before the image of the Virgin, together fusing voice, faith, and sentiment. This is a beautiful and salutary custom, from which certainly there cannot but be derived tranquility and abundance of heavenly gifts for the household.

– POPE PIUS XI

St. Teresa of the Andes, pray for us!

July 14

Never as in the rosary do the life of Jesus and that of Mary appear so deeply joined.

– ST. JOHN PAUL II

St. Kateri Tekakwitha, pray for us!

July 15

Many Christians have the custom of wearing the scapular; or they recall the central events in Christ's life by saying the rosary, never getting tired of repeating its words, just like people in love.

– St. Josemaría Escrivá

St. Clelia Barbieri, pray for us!

July 16

We come to Mary as perfect covenant partners, holding in one hand the sacrificial bowl, in the other the rosary, and invested with the scapular.

– Servant of God
(Fr.) Joseph Kentenich

Our Lady of Mt. Carmel, pray for us!

July 17

Among the various methods and forms of prayer
which are devoutly and profitably used in the
Catholic Church, that which is called the rosary
is for many reasons to be especially recommended.

– POPE LEO XIII

Blessed Marie-Geneviève Meunier, pray for us!

July 18

The one thing I want to do with my life is to devote
every minute of it to restoring the family rosary.

– SERVANT OF GOD
(FR.) PATRICK PEYTON

St. Camillus de Lellis, pray for us!

July 19

Those wander from the path of truth who
consider this devotion [the rosary] merely an
annoying formula repeated with monotonous
singsong intonation, and refuse it as good
only for children and silly women!

– POPE PIUS XI

Blessed Juliette Verolot, pray for us!

July 20

Humility is to the various virtues what the chain is
to the rosary: take away the chain and the
beads are scattered; remove humility
and all the virtues vanish.

– ST. JOHN VIANNEY

Blessed Marie-François Gabrielle Trézel, pray for us!

July 21

We honor [Mary] by praying the rosary with love
and devotion and by radiating her humility,
kindness, and thoughtfulness towards others.

– BLESSED TERESA OF CALCUTTA

St. Lawrence of Brindisi, pray for us!

July 22

A person who was leading an immoral life
had not the courage to give it up; he began
to say the rosary and was converted.

– ST. ALPHONSUS LIGUORI

Blessed Madeline-Claudine Ledoine, pray for us!

July 23

Arm yourselves with the arms of God — with the
holy rosary — and you will crush the devil's head and
you will stand firm in the face of all his temptations.
This is why even the material rosary itself is such a
terrible thing for the devil, and why the saints have
used it to enchain devils and to chase them out
of the bodies of people who were possessed.

– ST. LOUIS DE MONTFORT

Blessed Marie-Anne Piedcourt, pray for us

July 24

To understand the rosary, one has to enter into the
psychological dynamic proper to love.

– ST. JOHN PAUL II

St. Charbel Makhluf, pray for us!

July 25

When we have [said] the rosary at night ...
Christ is there with us.

– SERVANT OF GOD DOROTHY DAY

Blessed Maria Mercedes Prat, pray for us!

July 26

The rosary could very well be called the poem of
human redemption. The rosary is a poem that takes
its lively but simplistic hues from the pure palette of
the Gospel; while at the same time it draws its logical
ties, its harmonious responses, its entire intimate
dialectic from the highest theology.

– BLESSED BARTOLO LONGO

Sts. Joachim and Anne, pray for us!

July 27

The rosary is a good friend in joy, but an even better friend in battle. Today the drums continuously beat for battle. Our lives are one big battle. We are dependent on loyal, good friends. The rosary is such a good friend in the big battle of our time.

– SERVANT OF GOD (FR.) JOSEPH KENTENICH

Blessed Titus Brandsma, pray for us!

July 28

The single richest treasure in the Vatican is the rosary.

– BLESSED POPE PIUS IX

St. Alphonsa of the Immaculate Conception, pray for us!

July 29

When lovers are together, they spend hours and hours repeating the same thing: "I love you!" What is missing in the people who think the rosary monotonous is Love; and everything that is not done for love is worthless.

– SERVANT OF GOD LÚCIA DOS SANTOS

Blessed Paul Tcheng, pray for us!

July 30

We ardently desire that it [the rosary] be devoutly
continued and that the habit of the daily recitation of
the rosary in an alternating manner, so appreciated by
our forefathers and by them considered sacred for
the Christian family, be once again established.

– POPE PIUS XI

Blessed Maria Vicenta Chavez Orozco, pray for us!

July 31

It [the rosary] promotes the greater glory of God
because of the piety it produces among the people.

– ST. FRANCIS DE SALES

St. Ignatius of Loyola, pray for us!

AUGUST

August 1

The immense good that this noble devotion
[the rosary] has done to the world is well known.
How many, by its means, have been delivered
from sin! How many led to a holy life! How
many to a good death, and are now saved!

– ST. ALPHONSUS LIGUORI

St. Alphonsus Liguori, pray for us!

August 2

It must not be thought that the rosary is only for
women and for simple and ignorant people;
it is also for men and for the greatest of men.

– ST. LOUIS DE MONTFORT

St. Peter Julian Eymard, pray for us!

August 3

The rosary is a devotion that,
through the Blessed Mother,
leads us to Jesus.

– BLESSED POPE PAUL VI

Blessed Frédéric Jansoone, pray for us!

August 4

It is impossible to meditate with
devotion upon the mysteries of the rosary
and live in a state of sin.

– ST. JOHN VIANNEY

St. John Vianney, pray for us!

August 5

The rosary is the meeting ground of the
uneducated and the learned, the place where
the simple love grows in knowledge and
where the knowing mind grows in love.

– VENERABLE FULTON J. SHEEN

Blessed Miroslav Bulešić, pray for us!

August 6

If there was one inflexible rule in our home,
it was that every one of us had to participate
in the family rosary led by my father.

– SERVANT OF GOD
(FR.) PATRICK PEYTON

St. Mary MacKillop, pray for us!

August 7

The rosary helps us to be conformed ever more
closely to Christ until we attain true holiness.

– St. John Paul II

Blessed Edmund Bojanowski, pray for us!

August 8

Under her [Mary's] inspiration, strong with her might, great
men were raised up — illustrious for their sanctity no less
than for their apostolic spirit — to beat off the attacks of
wicked adversaries and to lead souls back into the virtuous
ways of Christian life, firing them with a consuming love
of the things of God. One such man, an army in himself,
was Dominic Guzman [St. Dominic]. Putting all his trust
in Our Lady's rosary, he set himself fearlessly to the
accomplishment of both these tasks with happy results.

– Pope Leo XIII

St. Dominic, pray for us!

August 9

Our need of divine help is as great today
as when the great Dominic introduced the use
of the rosary of Mary as a balm for the
wounds of his contemporaries.

— POPE LEO XIII

St. Teresa Benedicta of the Cross, pray for us!

August 10

We put great confidence in the holy rosary
for the healing of evils which afflict our times.
Not with force, not with arms, not with human
power, but with Divine help obtained
through the means of this prayer.

— VENERABLE POPE PIUS XII

Blessed Claudio Granzotto, pray for us!

August 11

The rosary has the power to convert even the most
hardened of hearts. I have known people who have gone
to missions and who have heard sermons on the most
terrifying subjects without being in the least moved;
and yet, after they had, on my advice, started to say the
rosary every day they eventually became converted
and gave themselves completely to God.

– St. Louis de Montfort

Blessed Karl Leisner, pray for us!

August 12

He [St. Francis de Sales] said his rosary
every day with quite extraordinary devotion.

– St. Jane Frances de Chantal

St. Jane Frances de Chantal, pray for us!

August 13

Does not a child call his mother all the time? His cry: "Mom!" is different according to the need that inspires and animates it. Therefore, recite the rosary like a child, invoking our Heavenly Mother and imploring her help.

– SERVANT OF GOD
(FR.) DOLINDO RUOTOLO

Blessed Isidore Bakanja, pray for us!

August 14

Behold, if we desire to rise even to her [Mary's] knowledge and loving of Jesus, we must whisper "Hail Mary," and repeating it, meditate upon these mysteries [of the rosary] in union with her.

– ST. MAXIMILIAN KOLBE

St. Maximilian Kolbe, pray for us!

August 15

When meditating on this glorious mystery
[the Assumption of Mary] during the recitation of
the rosary, or on seeing a picture of Our Lady being
assumed into Infinite Love, I think of that radiant
moment when I will see her, my Mother.

– BLESSED DINA BÉLANGER

Mary, Assumed into Heaven, pray for us!

August 16

The rosary is the prayer through which,
by repeating the angel's greeting to Mary,
we try to draw considerations of our own
on the mysteries of Redemption from
the Blessed Virgin's meditation.

– ST. JOHN PAUL II

Blessed Antoine-Frédéric Ozanam, pray for us!

August 17

This mystic crown [the rosary] not only is found
in and glides through the hands of the poor, but
it also is honored by citizens of every social rank.

– POPE PIUS XI

St. Jeanne Delanoue, pray for us!

August 18

When we say the rosary, which is a wonderful
devotion which I will never tire of recommending
to Christians everywhere, our minds and hearts
go over the mysteries of Mary's admirable life
which are, at the same time, the fundamental
mysteries of our faith.

– ST. JOSEMARÍA ESCRIVÁ

St. Alberto Hurtado, pray for us!

August 19

The origin of this form of prayer
[the rosary] is divine rather than human.

– POPE LEO XIII

St. John Eudes, pray for us!

August 20

The devils have an overwhelming fear of the rosary.
Saint Bernard says that the Angelic Salutation
puts them to flight and makes all hell tremble.

– ST. LOUIS DE MONTFORT

St. Bernard of Clairvaux, pray for us!

August 21

The rosary is the most beautiful and the richest
of all prayers to the Mediatrix of all grace;
it is the prayer that touches most the Heart
of the Mother of God. Say it each day!

– St. Pope Pius X

St. Pope Pius X, pray for us!

August 22

Sweet Queen of my heart, kindly accept the
prayer I address to you: that your love may
spread in my heart and in the hearts of all those
who honor you by reciting the blessed rosary.

– Blessed Bartolo Longo

Queen of Heaven, pray for us!

August 23

The rosary can be recited in full every day,
and there are those who most laudably do so.

— St. John Paul II

St. Rose of Lima, pray for us!

August 24

The rosary is a prayer which fits itself to changing
circumstances. At times of sickness or of exhaustion,
there is no other so useful.

— Servant of God Frank Duff

St. Joseph Calasanz, pray for us!

August 25

Saint Louis IX, King of France, recited the rosary
even while leading his army in time of war.

— Blessed James Alberione

St. Louis IX, pray for us!

August 26

The rosary is our good friend. Being familiar with it configures us to Christ. Through the rosary we become apparitions of Christ and encounters of Christ. How important a good friend is! A friend gives a child a sense of being sheltered even in a strange place. A good friend is a great treasure and a great rarity. Oh, the beautiful things that have been said and sung about friendship! And we may say and sing all this of the rosary, our good friend!

– SERVANT OF GOD
(FR.) JOSEPH KENTENICH

St. Teresa of Jesús Jornet, pray for us!

August 27

How often a rosary, a medal of the Blessed Mother, devout novenas, [or] penances for the salvation of obstinate sinners who are ill have obtained real prodigies from this Mother!

– BLESSED JAMES ALBERIONE

St. Monica, pray for us!

August 28

Everyone can understand how salutary it [the rosary] is, especially in our times wherein sometimes a certain annoyance of the things of the spirit is felt even among the faithful, and a dislike, as it were, for the Christian doctrine.

– POPE PIUS XI

St. Augustine, pray for us!

August 29

As the various mysteries present themselves one after the other in the formula of the rosary for the meditation and contemplation of men's minds, they also elucidate what we owe to Mary for our reconciliation and salvation.

– POPE LEO XIII

Blessed Laurentia Kerasymiv, pray for us!

August 30

I urge you all to recite the rosary every day,
abandoning yourselves with trust in Mary's hands.

– POPE BENEDICT XVI

Blessed Alfredo Ildefonso Schuster, pray for us!

August 31

The formula of the rosary … is excellently adapted to prayer in
common, so that it has been styled, not without reason,
"The Psalter of Mary." And that old custom of our forefathers
ought to be preserved or else restored, according to which
Christian families, whether in town or country, were religiously
wont at close of day, when their labors were at an end, to
assemble before a figure of Our Lady and alternately recite the
rosary. She, delighted at this faithful and unanimous homage,
was ever near them like a loving mother surrounded by her
children, distributing to them the blessings of domestic
peace, the foretaste of the peace of heaven.

– POPE LEO XIII

Blessed Diego Ventaja Milán, pray for us!

SEPTEMBER

September 1

The rosary in particular is a sign of predestination.
Our fidelity in reciting it is a sure sign of salvation.

– Blessed Alan de la Roche

Blessed Alan de la Roche, pray for us!

September 2

At times when Christianity itself seemed under threat, its
deliverance was attributed to the power of this prayer
[the rosary], and Our Lady of the Rosary was acclaimed
as the one whose intercession brought salvation.

– St. John Paul II

Blessed Anthony Ishida, pray for us!

September 3

As the magnifying glass catches and unites the
scattered rays of the sun, so the rosary brings
together the otherwise dissipated thoughts of
life in the sickroom into the white and
burning heat of Divine Love.

— VENERABLE FULTON J. SHEEN

Blessed Brigida of Jesus, pray for us!

September 4

A person who maintained a sinful friendship,
by saying the rosary felt a horror of sin; she fell
a few more times into sin, but by means
of the rosary was soon quite converted.

— ST. ALPHONSUS LIGUORI

Blessed Dina Bélanger, pray for us!

September 5

The other day I can't tell you how bad I felt —
there was a moment when I nearly refused to accept
— deliberately I took the rosary and very slowly
without even meditating or thinking — I said it
slowly and calmly — the moment passed —
but the darkness is so dark, and the pain is so painful
— but I accept whatever he [Jesus] gives
and I give whatever he takes.

– BLESSED TERESA OF CALCUTTA

Blessed Teresa of Calcutta, pray for us!

September 6

The rosary is the glory of
the Roman Church.

– ST. POPE JOHN XXIII

Blessed Odoardo Focherini, pray for us!

September 7

To those therefore who are striving after supreme happiness,
this means of the rosary has been most providentially
offered, and it is one unsurpassed for facility and
convenience. For any person even moderately instructed
in his religion can make use of it with fruit, and the
time it occupies cannot delay any man's business.

– POPE LEO XIII

Blessed Eugenia Picco, pray for us!

September 8

You show your devotion to Mary by celebrating
her feasts, by daily prayer in her honor and especially
the rosary, and by imitating her life. May that
devotion grow stronger every day.

– ST. JOHN PAUL II

Blessed Dominic of Nagasaki, pray for us!

September 9

People are often quite unaware of how rich the rosary
is in indulgences. This is because many priests,
when preaching on the rosary, hardly ever mention
indulgences and give rather a flowery and
popular sermon which excites admiration
but scarcely teaches anything.

— ST. LOUIS DE MONTFORT

St. Peter Claver, pray for us!

September 10

What fruits the world and
the Church owe to the rosary!

— SERVANT OF GOD
(FR.) JOSEPH KENTENICH

Blessed Pierre Bonhomme, pray for us!

September 11

In the present international situation,
I appeal to all – individuals, families, and
communities – to pray the rosary for peace,
even daily, so that the world will be preserved
from the dreadful scourge of terrorism.

– St. John Paul II

St. John-Gabriel Perboyre, pray for us!

September 12

From the fact that this warfare of prayer [the rosary] is "enrolled
under the name of the Mother of God," fresh efficacy and fresh
honor are thereby added to it. Hence the frequent repetition in
the rosary of the "Hail Mary" after each "Our Father." So far
from this derogating in any way from the honor due to God, as
though it indicated that we placed greater confidence in Mary's
patronage than in God's power, it is rather this which
especially moves God, and wins his mercy for us.

– Pope Leo XIII

Blessed Thomas Zumarraga, pray for us!

September 13

Stir up your confidence in the Holy Virgin of the rosary!
You should have the faith of Job! Beloved Holy Mother,
I place in you all my sorrows, all my hopes,
and all my confidence!

– BLESSED BARTOLO LONGO

Blessed Paolo Manna, pray for us!

September 14

In moments when fever, agony, and pain make it hard to
pray, the suggestion of prayer that comes from merely
holding the rosary — or better still, from caressing the
Crucifix at the end of it — is tremendous.

– VENERABLE FULTON J. SHEEN

St. John Chrysostom, pray for us!

September 15

For in the rosary all the part that Mary took
as our Co-Redemptress comes to us.

– POPE LEO XIII

Our Lady of Sorrows, pray for us!

September 16

Pray the holy rosary. Blessed be that
monotony of Hail Marys which purifies
the monotony of your sins!

– ST. JOSEMARÍA ESCRIVÁ

Blessed Carlo Eraña Guruceta, pray for us!

September 17

Amidst all prayers, the rosary is the most
beautiful, the richest in graces, and the one
that most pleases the Most Holy Virgin.

– ST. POPE PIUS X

St. Robert Bellarmine, pray for us!

September 18

When I am sad, here is my cure: I say the
glorious mysteries of the rosary, and I tell myself,
"After all, what difference does it make if I am
poor, and nothing comes of the good I hope for?
None of that keeps our beloved Jesus — who wants
the good a thousand times more than I — from
being blessed, eternally and infinitely blessed."

– BLESSED CHARLES DE FOUCAULD

St. Joseph of Cupertino, pray for us!

September 19

If you recite the family rosary, all united,
you shall taste peace; you shall have
in your homes concord of souls.

– VENERABLE POPE PIUS XII

St. Agatha Yi, pray for us!

September 20

To what ends does not the evil one go against us while
we are engaged in saying our rosary against him. Being
human, we easily become tired and slipshod — but the
devil makes these difficulties worse when we are saying
the rosary. Before we even begin he makes us feel bored,
distracted, or exhausted — and when we have started
praying he oppresses us from all sides.

– ST. LOUIS DE MONTFORT

St. Paul Chong Hasang, pray for us!

September 21

The rosary has a peaceful effect
on those who pray it.

– St. John Paul II

St. François Jaccard, pray for us!

September 22

As we say the rosary, we try to stage the mysteries before
our minds. However meager our powers to meditate,
we cannot help learning all those mysteries. They expand
into so many "photographic" situations, linking themselves up with the various pictures we have seen or the
accounts which we have heard or read of those events.
    We may be sure too that grace takes hold of that
"picturisation," intensifies it and renders it fruitful.

– Servant of God Frank Duff

St. Thomas of Villanova, pray for us!

September 23

Love Our Lady and help others to love her.
Always recite the rosary.

– ST. PADRE PIO

St. Padre Pio, pray for us!

September 24

At one time this prayer [the rosary] was particularly
dear to Christian families, and it certainly brought
them closer together. It is important not to lose
this precious inheritance. We need to return to
the practice of family prayer and prayer
for families, continuing to use the rosary.

– ST. JOHN PAUL II

St. Anton Martin Slomšek, pray for us!

September 25

The rosary is a miraculous means;
the most capable one amongst other means,
to destroy sin and regain divine grace.

– POPE GREGORY XVI

Blessed Louis Tezza, pray for us!

September 26

Pronounce the Our Father and the Hail Marys of
each decade [of the rosary] clearly and without
rushing: this will help you always to get more
and more out of this way of loving Mary.

– ST. JOSEMARÍA ESCRIVÁ

St. Thérèse Couderc, pray for us!

September 27

Give me time to say the rosary and I guarantee
you I shall convert any dying patient,
no matter how much he may refuse.

– St. Clement Hofbauer

St. Vincent de Paul, pray for us!

September 28

Without interruption he [St. Simón de Rojas]
repeated the invocation and greeting "Hail Mary"
so that, very frequently, he was affectionately
called "Father Hail Mary." He did much to
make known the prayer of the holy rosary.

– St. John Paul II

St. Simón de Rojas, pray for us!

September 29

As often as, in reciting the rosary, we meditate upon the mysteries of our Redemption, so often do we in a manner emulate the sacred duties once committed to the Angelic hosts.

– POPE LEO XIII

Sts. Michael, Gabriel and Raphael, pray for us!

September 30

To pray the rosary for children, and even more, with children, training them from their earliest years to experience this daily "pause for prayer" with the family, is admittedly not the solution to every problem, but it is a spiritual aid which should not be underestimated.

– ST. JOHN PAUL II

St. Theodora Guérin, pray for us!

OCTOBER

October 1

I feel that I say the rosary so poorly!
I make a concentrated effort to meditate on the
mysteries of the rosary, but I am unable to focus my
concentration. For a long time I was disconsolate
about my lack of devotion, which astonished me since
I so much loved the Blessed Virgin that it ought to
have been easy for me to recite the prayers in her
honor that so much pleased her. But now I am less
sad, for I think that the Queen of Heaven, who is
also my Mother, ought to see my good intentions
and that she is pleased with them.

– St. Thérèse of Lisieux

St. Thérèse of Lisieux, pray for us!

October 2

When I went to the garden one afternoon, my
Guardian Angel said to me, "Pray for the dying."
And so I began at once to pray the rosary
with the gardeners for the dying.

– St. Faustina Kowalska

Holy Guardian Angels, pray for us!

October 3

If ever I come to the end of a day without having said
the rosary, I confess that I feel disappointed.

– Blessed Columba Marmion

Blessed Columba Marmion, pray for us!

October 4

Praying the rosary together, as a family, is very
beautiful and a source of great strength!

– Pope Francis

St. Francis of Assisi, pray for us!

October 5

O blessed rosary of Mary, sweet chain which
binds us to God, bond of love which unites
us to the angels, tower of salvation against the
assaults of hell, safe port in our universal
shipwreck, we shall never abandon you.

– BLESSED BARTOLO LONGO

Blessed Bartolo Longo, pray for us!

October 6

The power of the rosary
is beyond description.

– VENERABLE FULTON J. SHEEN

St. Faustina Kowalska, pray for us!

October 7

Our Lady invites us every year to rediscover
the beauty of this prayer [the rosary],
so simple and so profound.

– POPE BENEDICT XVI

Our Lady of the Rosary, pray for us!

October 8

While respecting the freedom of the children of
God, the Church has always proposed certain
practices of piety to the faithful with particular
solicitude and insistence. Among these should
be mentioned the recitation of the rosary.

– ST. JOHN PAUL II

Blessed Marie-Rose Durocher, pray for us!

October 9

Now the great power of the rosary lies in this,
that it makes the Creed into a prayer; of course,
the Creed is in some sense a prayer and a great act
of homage to God; but the rosary gives us the great
truths of his life and death to meditate upon,
and brings them nearer to our hearts.

– BLESSED JOHN HENRY NEWMAN

Blessed John Henry Newman, pray for us!

October 10

The rosary, if rightly considered, will be found to
have in itself special virtues, whether for producing and
continuing a state of recollection, or for touching the
conscience for its healing, or for lifting up the soul.

– POPE LEO XIII

Blessed Diego Luis de San Vitores, pray for us!

October 11

Oh, what a delight this blessed rosary is!
Oh, what assurance it brings of being heard
here on earth and in the eternal heavens!

– ST. POPE JOHN XXIII

St. Pope John XXIII, pray for us!

October 12

They will be true apostles of the latter times to whom
the Lord of Hosts will give eloquence and strength to
work wonders and carry off glorious spoils from his
enemies. … [T]hey will carry the crucifix in their
right hand and the rosary in their left, and the holy
names of Jesus and Mary on their heart.

– ST. LOUIS DE MONTFORT

St. Daniel Comboni, pray for us!

October 13

I am the Lady of the Rosary.

– OUR LADY OF FATIMA

Our Lady of Fatima, pray for us!

October 14

We must be strong and prepared and trust in
Christ and in his Holy Mother and be very,
very assiduous in praying the holy rosary.

– ST. JOHN PAUL II

*Blessed Alexandrina Maria
da Costa, pray for us!*

October 15

I rise as early as possible each morning, as soon as the
alarm rings; a half-hour of meditation every day, not to
be neglected except for circumstances out of my control;
half an hour at least dedicated to spiritual reading;
Mass every morning and Holy Communion as regularly
as possible; confession once a week normally and
frequent spiritual direction; daily recitation
of the rosary and the *Angelus* at noon.

– BLESSED ALBERTO MARVELLI

St. Teresa of Avila, pray for us!

October 16

For we are convinced that the rosary,
if devoutly used, is bound to benefit not
only the individual but society at large.

– POPE LEO XIII

St. Gerard Majella, pray for us!

October 17

The holy rosary not only serves admirably to overcome
the enemies of God and Religion, but is also a stimulus
and spur to the practice of evangelical virtues which it
injects and cultivates in our souls. Above all, it nourishes
the Catholic Faith, which flourishes again by due
meditation on the sacred mysteries, and raises
minds to the truth revealed to us by God.

– POPE PIUS XI

St. Margaret Mary Alacoque, pray for us!

October 18

Take [up] the rosary, one of the most deeply
rooted of Christian devotions. The Church
encourages us to contemplate its mysteries.

– ST. JOSEMARÍA ESCRIVÁ

St. Luke the Evangelist, pray for us!

October 19

The prayer of the rosary is perfect,
because of the praises it offers, the lessons
it teaches, the graces it obtains,
and the victories it achieves.

– POPE BENEDICT XV

St. Charles Garnier, pray for us!

October 20

The rosary should be said with
great devotion because you are speaking
to the Most Holy Virgin, the Mother of God.

– ST. PAUL OF THE CROSS

St. Paul of the Cross, pray for us!

October 21

Please do not scorn this beautiful and
heavenly tree, but plant it with your hands
in the garden of your soul, making the
resolution to say your rosary every day.

– ST. LOUIS DE MONTFORT

Blessed Giuseppe Puglisi, pray for us!

October 22

The rosary is my
favorite prayer.

– ST. JOHN PAUL II

St. John Paul II, pray for us!

October 23

The rosary is the most complete and easiest instruction about the Blessed Mother, and it is the source of devotion to the Divine Master.

– BLESSED TIMOTHY GIACCARDO

Blessed Timothy Giaccardo, pray for us!

October 24

When people love and recite the rosary they find it makes them better.

– ST. ANTHONY MARY CLARET

St. Anthony Mary Claret, pray for us!

October 25

Say the rosary every day.

– BLESSED FRANCIS XAVIER SEELOS

Blessed Nicolas Barré, pray for us!

October 26

In the 19th century she [Blessed Ann Maria Adorni] was an exemplary wife and mother and then, widowed, she devoted herself to charity to women in prison and in difficulty, for whose service she founded two religious Institutes. Because of her ceaseless prayer, Mother Adorni was known as the "Living Rosary."

– POPE BENEDICT XVI

Blessed Anna Maria Adorni, pray for us!

October 27

As the history of the Church makes clear, this very fruitful way of praying [the rosary] is not only efficacious in warding off evils and preventing calamities, but is also of great help in fostering Christian life.

– BLESSED POPE PAUL VI

St. Gaetano Errico, pray for us!

October 28

There are several ways of saying the holy rosary,
but that which gives Almighty God the greatest glory,
does the most for our souls and which the devil
fears more than any other, is that of saying or
chanting the rosary publicly in two groups.

– St. Louis de Montfort

Blessed Maria Restituta Kafka, pray for us!

October 29

I am pleading with you to become apostles of the
rosary. Promote the rosary. Urge the rosary.
Teach the rosary. Shall I say, advertise the rosary.
It is through the rosary that we can bring countless
souls back to Christ from whom they have strayed.
It is through the rosary that we can make them lovers
of Christ through the mediation of his Mother.

– Servant of God (Fr.) John Hardon

Blessed Chiara Luce Badano, pray for us!

October 30

May Mary, the Mother of God and of men,
herself the authoress and teacher of the rosary,
procure for us its happy fulfillment.

– POPE LEO XIII

Blessed Jean-Michel Langevin, pray for us!

October 31

As I pondered over my condition [Bartolo Long had
been a Satanist], I experienced a deep sense of despair
and almost committed suicide. Then I heard an echo
in my ear of the voice of Friar Alberto repeating the
words of the Blessed Virgin Mary: "If you seek
salvation, promulgate the rosary. This is Mary's own
promise." These words illumined my soul. I went on
my knees. "If it is true, I will not leave this valley
until I have propagated your rosary."

– BLESSED BARTOLO LONGO

St. Valentín Berrio-Ochoa, pray for us!

NOVEMBER

November 1

Saint Pius V, one of the greatest Popes who ever ruled
the Church, said the rosary every day. Saint Thomas of
Villanova, Archbishop of Valence, St. Ignatius, St. Francis
Xavier, St. Francis Borgia, St. Theresa, and St. Philip Neri,
as well as many other great men whom I have not
mentioned were deeply devoted to the holy rosary.

– St. Louis de Montfort

All Saints, pray for us!

November 2

If we want to help the souls in purgatory,
then we should say the rosary for them
because the rosary gives them great relief.

– St. Alphonsus de Liguori

Blessed Josefa Naval Girbés, pray for us!

November 3

I will never allow myself the least license in my exercises of piety, my morning and night prayers, daily meditations, liturgical prayers, frequent communions, rosary (at least one decade), the gift of all the indulgences gained during the day to the souls in Purgatory, and the offering of the day's works and sufferings for particular intentions, for the welfare of souls or of the Church.

– SERVANT OF GOD ELISABETH LESEUR

Blessed Aimée-Adèle le Bouteiller, pray for us!

November 4

Let us follow the footsteps of all those true servants of Mary. Belonging to this number was St. Charles Borromeo, who always said his rosary on his knees.

– ST. JOHN VIANNEY

St. Charles Borromeo, pray for us!

November 5

Turn to Mary most holy, your heavenly Mother;
pray to her with fervor, especially by means
of the rosary; invoke her daily in order to be
authentic imitators of Christ in our day.

– ST. JOHN PAUL II

St. Guido Maria Conforti, pray for us!

November 6

The spirit of prayer and the practice
of Christian life are best attained through
the devotion of the rosary of Mary.

– POPE LEO XIII

Blessed Anthony Baldinucci, pray for us!

November 7

Every word of the rosary
is a prayer to God.

– SERVANT OF GOD FRANK DUFF

Blessed Elizabeth of the Trinity, pray for us!

November 8

Whoever meditates on the mysteries of the rosary and
contemplates the examples of total sacrifice and
boundless charity proffered by our Lord Jesus Christ
and his Mother in their supreme ideal of glorifying
God and saving the world, must feel impelled to
orientate his life in such a way that the sublime
message of the Our Father and the Hail Mary, as
well as the benefits of the Annunciation, Calvary
and Pentecost, may reach the greatest possible
number of souls abundantly and rapidly.

– ST. POPE JOHN XXIII

Blessed Maria Crucified Satellico, pray for us!

November 9

What a wonderful thing to have Jesus Christ
in our midst! And the only thing we have to do to
get him to come is to say the rosary in a group.

– St. Louis de Montfort

Blessed Eugene Bossilkov, pray for us!

November 10

Dear brothers and sisters, recite the rosary every
day. I earnestly urge pastors to pray the rosary and
to teach people in the Christian communities how to
pray it. For the faithful and courageous fulfillment of
the human and Christian duties proper to each
one's state, help the people of God to return
to the daily recitation of the rosary.

– St. John Paul II

St. Gregory Palamas, pray for us!

November 11

We now desire, as a continuation of the thought
of our predecessors, to recommend strongly
the recitation of the family rosary.

– BLESSED POPE PAUL VI

Blessed Kamen Vitchev, pray for us!

November 12

The rosary counteracts any
tendency to relegate her [Mary] to a
sub-compartment in the Christian life.

– SERVANT OF GOD FRANK DUFF

Blessed Gregory Lakota, pray for us!

November 13

He [St. Stanislaus Kostka] never did anything without first turning to her [Mary's] image to ask her blessing. When he said her office, the rosary, or other prayers, he did so with the same external marks of affection as he would have done had he been speaking face to face with Mary.

– St. Alphonsus Liguori

St. Stanislaus Kostka, pray for us!

November 14

Confidently take up the rosary once again. Rediscover the rosary in light of Scripture, in harmony with the liturgy, and in the context of your daily lives. May this appeal of mine not go unheard!

– St. John Paul II

St. Frances Xavier Cabrini, pray for us!

November 15

After the Sacred Liturgy of the Eucharist,
the prayer of the rosary is what best fosters
within our spirit the growth of the
mysteries of faith, hope, and charity.

– SERVANT OF GOD LÚCIA DOS SANTOS

Blessed Josaphat Kotsylovsky, pray for us!

November 16

When we feel weary of life and all its problems,
let us pick up the rosary.

– SERVANT OF GOD RAFAEL
(CARDINAL) MERRY DEL VAL

St. Giuseppe Moscati, pray for us!

November 17

Somebody who says his rosary alone only gains the
merit of one rosary, but if he says it together with
thirty other people he gains the merit of thirty
rosaries. This is the law of public prayer.
How profitable, how advantageous this is!

– St. Louis de Montfort

St. Roque González de Santa Cruz, pray for us!

November 18

In places, families, and nations in which the
rosary of Mary retains its ancient honor,
the loss of faith through ignorance and
vicious error need not be feared.

– Pope Leo XIII

St. Rose Philippine Duchesne, pray for us!

November 19

Anyone who says the rosary will have a
reasonably complete and vivid idea
of the Christian narrative.

– SERVANT OF GOD FRANK DUFF

Blessed Karolina Kózka, pray for us!

November 20

If the rosary is such an efficacious and convenient way for
individuals to communicate with God and win such an
abundance of graces through the invaluable intercession
of the Blessed Virgin, we are persuaded that families will
receive from this salutary form of prayer a guarantee of
heavenly blessings, while at the same time they will find in
the rosary a school in which to form themselves in virtue.

– ST. POPE JOHN XXIII

Blessed Salvatore Lilli, pray for us!

November 21

The rosary elevates minds to the truths revealed
by God and shows us Heaven opened. The Virgin
Mary herself has insistently recommended this
manner of praying. All graces are conceded
to us by God through the hands of Mary.

– POPE PIUS XI

Blessed Franciszka Siedliska, pray for us!

November 22

Those who pray the rosary do more for the benefit
of the whole human race than all the orators and
deputies, more than all the organizers, secretaries
and writers, more than all the capitalists
even if they would make their entire
wealth available to the Church.

– SERVANT OF GOD (FR.) JOSEPH KENTENICH

Blessed Toros Oghlou David, pray for us!

November 23

Pause for a few seconds — three or four — in silent
meditation to consider each mystery of the rosary
before you recite the Our Father and the Hail Marys
of that decade. I am sure this practice will increase
you recollection and the fruits of your prayer.

– St. Josemaría Escrivá

Blessed Miguel Agustin Pro, pray for us!

November 24

I want the rosary said every day
with as much love as possible.

– St. Francis de Sales

Blessed Maria Anna Sala, pray for us!

November 25

Drawing on the word of God and the witness of the saints, the blessed couple [Blesseds Luigi and Maria Beltrame Quattrocchi] lived an ordinary life in an extraordinary way. Among the joys and anxieties of a normal family, they knew how to live an extraordinarily rich spiritual life. At the center of their life was the daily Eucharist as well as devotion to the Virgin Mary, to whom they prayed every evening with the rosary.

– ST. JOHN PAUL II

Blesseds Luigi and
Maria Beltrame Quattrocchi, pray for us!

November 26

Let us recite the holy rosary
often and well.

– BLESSED JAMES ALBERIONE

Blessed James Alberione, pray for us!

November 27

Saint John Berchmans died clutching the crucifix,
the rosary, and the rules of his order. "These were
the three things dearest to me during my life,"
he kept saying, "with these I die happily."

— BLESSED JAMES ALBERIONE

St. John Berchmans, pray for us!

November 28

My God, you did not look at my past, you did not
stop before my weakness; in one hand you placed the
rosary, in the other a pen, and you said to me:
"Write, they will listen to you, for it is I who will
place in your heart the word of life."

— BLESSED BARTOLO LONGO

St. Catherine Labouré, pray for us!

November 29

The holy rosary offers us a summary of the Gospel,
and leads us, in an easy and accessible way,
to prayer from the heart.

– St. John Paul II

St. Leonard of Port Maurice, pray for us!

November 30

The Most Holy Virgin, in these last times in which we
live, has given a new efficacy to the recitation of the
rosary to such an extent that there is no problem, no
matter how difficult it is, whether temporal or above all
spiritual, in the personal life of each one of us, of our
families … that cannot be solved by the rosary. There is
no problem, I tell you, no matter how difficult it is, that
we cannot resolve by the prayer of the holy rosary.

– Servant of God Lúcia Dos Santos

St. Joseph Marchand, pray for us!

December 1

The rosary is a prayer of repetition.
Father [Blessed Charles] de Foucauld said,
"Love is expressed with few words, always
the same and always repeated."

– SERVANT OF GOD POPE JOHN PAUL I

Blessed Charles de Foucauld, pray for us!

December 2

We exhort all Catholic families to introduce
this devotion [the rosary] into their lives,
and to encourage its propagation.

– BLESSED POPE PAUL VI

St. Edmund Campion, pray for us!

December 3

Of all forms of prayer, that of the rosary is more than
ever necessary, for it not only addresses itself to Mary,
through whom it pleased God to send every grace
to us, but more than any other prayer, it bears the
universal stamp of collective and familial prayer.

– POPE BENEDICT XV

*Blessed Marie-Clémentine
Anuarite Nengapeta, pray for us!*

December 4

If a church or a chapel is not available,
say the rosary together in your own
or a neighbor's house.

– ST. LOUIS DE MONTFORT

St. Giovanni Calabria, pray for us!

December 5

Even though it costs me a lot to pray,
I pray the rosary every day.

– VENERABLE FAUSTINO
PEREZ-MANGLANO

Blessed Philip Rinaldi, pray for us!

December 6

Through the rosary we allow ourselves to be
guided by Mary, the model of faith, in meditating
on the mysteries of Christ. Day after day she helps
us to assimilate the Gospel, so that it gives
a form to our life as a whole.

– POPE BENEDICT XVI

Blessed Adolph Kolping, pray for us!

December 7

The rosary of the Blessed Virgin Mary,
combining in a convenient and practical form
an unexcelled form of prayer, an instrument well
adapted to preserve the faith and an illustrious
example of perfect virtue, should be often in the
hands of the true Christian and be devoutly
recited and meditated upon.

– POPE LEO XIII

Blessed John Duns Scotus, pray for us!

December 8

With Mary Immaculate, the faithful handmaid of
the Lord, and under the guidance of the Spirit,
we enter into closer union with Jesus Christ. We
will contemplate with her the mysteries of the
Incarnate Word, especially in praying the rosary.

– ST. EUGÈNE DE MAZENOD

Immaculate Mary, pray for us!

December 9

All people of good will can, and must,
say the rosary every day.

– SERVANT OF GOD LÚCIA DOS SANTOS

St. Juan Diego, pray for us!

December 10

I renounce all the distractions I may have
during this rosary which I wish to say with
modesty, attention, and devotion, just as
if it were to be the last of my life.

– ST. LOUIS DE MONTFORT

Blessed Marcantonio Durando, pray for us!

December 11

May the example of Blessed Ladislaus (László)
Batthyány-Strattmann, who prayed the
rosary daily with his family, strengthen
you in your veneration of Our Lady.

– ST. JOHN PAUL II

Blessed László Batthyány-Strattmann, pray for us!

December 12

Toward Mary we must have an enlightened and
limitless confidence and love; the most heartfelt,
expansive, and tender devotion; the most common
and constant practices of the rosary, the *Angelus*,
the three Hail Marys, the chaplet, Saturday, etc.

– BLESSED JAMES ALBERIONE

Our Lady of Guadalupe, pray for us!

December 13

Go to Mass and Communion often;
try to say the rosary every day, and, above all,
increase your love for Our Blessed Lady.

– VENERABLE TERESA OF JESUS QUEVEDO

Blessed José María of Manila, pray for us!

December 14

Among the several rites and manners of
paying honor to the Blessed Mary, some are
to be preferred, inasmuch as we know them
to be most powerful and most pleasing to our
Mother; and for this reason we specially
mention by name and recommend the rosary.

– POPE LEO XIII

St. Nimatullah Kassab Al-Hardini, pray for us!

December 15

The rosary should be
recited reverently.

– SERVANT OF GOD FRANK DUFF

St. Virginia Bracelli, pray for us!

December 16

To be apostles of the rosary, it is necessary to
experience personally the beauty and depth of this
prayer which is simple and accessible to everyone.
It is first of all necessary to let the Blessed Virgin
Mary take one by the hand to contemplate
the Face of Christ: a joyful, luminous,
sorrowful and glorious face.

– POPE BENEDICT XVI

Blessed Clemente Marchisio, pray for us!

December 17

The mind is infinitely variable in its language, but the heart is not. The heart of a man, in the face of the woman he loves, is too poor to translate the infinity of his affection into a different word. So the heart takes one expression, "I love you," and in saying it over and over again, it never repeats. That is what we do when we say the rosary — we are saying to God, the Trinity, to the Incarnate Savior, to the Blessed Mother: "I love you, I love you, I love you."

– VENERABLE FULTON J. SHEEN

St. José Manyanet y Vives, pray for us!

December 18

What is so good about the rosary is that it goes all the way in telling the whole story of Jesus and Mary and ourselves.

– SERVANT OF GOD (FR.) PATRICK PEYTON

Blessed María Inés Teresa del Santísimo Sacramento, pray for us!

December 19

Our most lively and sure hope is placed
in the Queen of the Rosary, who has shown
herself, since she has been invoked by that
title, so ready to help the Church and
Christian peoples in their necessities.

– POPE LEO XIII

Blessed Maria Fortunata Viti, pray for us!

December 20

Through your own personal experience
of the beauty of the rosary, may you
come to promote it with conviction.

– ST. JOHN PAUL II

St. Ephrem the Syrian, pray for us!

December 21

Let us live the rosary and
we shall live the Gospel!

– St. Luigi Orione

Blessed Peter Friedhofen, pray for us!

December 22

The rosary relates the
Christian life to that of Mary.

– Venerable Fulton J. Sheen

Blessed María Crescencia Pérez, pray for us!

December 23

The rosary is a compendium of the Holy Gospel;
it is a summary of the lives of our Lord
and the Virgin Mary; it is a summary
of the entirety of Christian doctrine.

– BLESSED JAMES ALBERIONE

Blessed Pope Paul VI, pray for us!

December 24

Each of Christ's mysteries is a revelation of his virtues.
The humility of the crib, the retirement of his hidden
life, the zeal of his public life, the self-annihilation of his
sacrifice, the glory of his triumph; all these disclose
virtues which we must imitate; they are mysteries in
which we should participate. This is the reason why the
contemplation of the mysteries of Christ — for instance,
while reciting the rosary — is so fruitful for the soul.

– BLESSED COLUMBA MARMION

St. Toribio Romo González, pray for us!

December 25

The rosary is a great test of faith. What the Eucharist is in the order of Sacraments, that the rosary is in order of sacramentals — the mystery and the test of faith, the touchstone by which the soul is judged in its humility. The mark of the Christian is the willingness to look for the Divine in the flesh of a babe in a crib, the continuing [presence of] Christ under the appearance of bread on an altar, and a meditation and a prayer on a string of beads.

– VENERABLE FULTON J. SHEEN

Blessed Michael Nakashima, pray for us!

December 26

Let's say the rosary!

– VENERABLE SOLANUS CASEY

Blessed Albertina Berkenbrock, pray for us!

December 27

If you want to live a holy life, cultivate devotion to Mary in your family. Gather your children in prayer and in the recitation of the holy rosary.

– SERVANT OF GOD
(FR.) DOLINDO RUOTOLO

St. John the Apostle, pray for us!

December 28

You [Mary] are omnipotent by grace and therefore you can help us. Were you not willing to help us, since we are ungrateful children and undeserving of your protection, we would not know to whom to turn. Your motherly Heart would not permit you to see us, your children, lost. The Infant whom we see on your knees and the blessed rosary which we see in your hand inspire confidence in us that we shall be heard.

– BLESSED BARTOLO LONGO

Blessed Laura Vicuña, pray for us!

December 29

At whom is the Virgin Mary looking? She is looking
at each and every one of us. And how does she look
at us? She looks at us as a Mother, with tenderness,
mercy, and love. That was how she gazed at
her Son Jesus at all the moments of his life
— Joyful, Luminous, Sorrowful, Glorious
— as we contemplate in the mysteries of the
holy rosary, simply and lovingly.

– POPE FRANCIS

St. Thomas Becket, pray for us!

December 30

The rosary mystically transports us to
Mary's side as she is busy watching over the
human growth of Christ in the home of Nazareth.

– ST. JOHN PAUL II

St. John Alcober, pray for us!

December 31

Suffice it to know that this devotion
[the rosary] has been approved by the Church,
and that the Sovereign Pontiffs have
enriched it with indulgences.

– St. Alphonsus Liguori

Blessed Álvaro del Portillo, pray for us!

HOW TO PRAY THE ROSARY

1. Make the Sign of the Cross and pray the "Apostles' Creed."
   (All Rosary Prayers, such as the Apostles Creed, can be found in the next section.)

2. Pray the "Our Father."

3. Pray three "Hail Marys."

4. Pray the "Glory be to the Father."

5. Announce the First Mystery; then Pray the "Our Father."

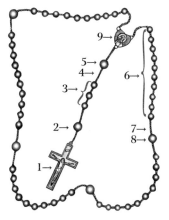

6. Pray 10 "Hail Marys" while meditating on the Mystery.

7. Pray the "Glory be to the Father" followed by the prayer requested by Our Lady of Fatima: "O my Jesus, forgive us our sins, save us from the fires of hell, lead all souls to Heaven, especially those in most need of Thy mercy."

8. Announce the Second Mystery. Then pray the "Our Father." Repeat 6 and 7 and continue with the Third, Fourth, and Fifth Mysteries in the same manner.

9. Pray the "Hail, Holy Queen" on the medal after the five decades are completed.

10. Pray the optional closing prayer, if you wish, and then make the Sign of the Cross.

Rosary Prayers

The Sign of the Cross

In the name of the Father, and of the Son, and of the Holy Spirit. Amen.

The Apostles' Creed

I believe in God, the Father almighty, Creator of heaven and earth, and in Jesus Christ, his only Son, our Lord, who was conceived by the Holy Spirit, born of the Virgin Mary, suffered under Pontius Pilate, was crucified, died, and was buried; he descended into hell; on the third day he rose again from the dead; he ascended into heaven, and is seated at the right hand of God the Father almighty; from there he will come to judge the living and the dead. I believe in the Holy Spirit, the holy catholic Church, the communion of saints, the forgiveness of sins, the resurrection of the body, and life everlasting. Amen.

Our Father

Our Father, who art in heaven, hallowed be Thy name; Thy kingdom come; Thy will be done on earth, as it is in heaven. Give us this day our daily bread; and forgive us our trespasses, as we forgive those who trespass against us; and lead us not into temptation, but deliver us from evil. Amen.

Hail Mary

Hail, Mary, full of grace; the Lord is with thee; blessed art thou among women, and blessed is the fruit of thy womb, Jesus. Holy Mary, Mother of God, pray for us sinners, now and at the hour of our death. Amen.

Glory Be

Glory be to the Father, and to the Son, and to the Holy Spirit. As it was in the beginning, is now, and ever shall be, world without end. Amen.

Fatima Prayer

O my Jesus, forgive us our sins, save us from the fires of hell. Lead all souls to Heaven, especially those in most need of Thy mercy.

Hail, Holy Queen

Hail, Holy Queen, Mother of Mercy, our life, our sweetness, and our hope. To thee do we cry, poor banished children of Eve; to thee do we send up our sighs, mourning and weeping in this valley of tears. Turn then, most gracious advocate, thine eyes of mercy toward us; and after this our exile show unto us the blessed fruit of thy womb, Jesus. O clement, O loving, O sweet Virgin Mary.

V. Pray for us, O holy Mother of God.
R. That we may be made worthy of the promises of Christ.

Optional Closing Prayer

O God, whose only-begotten Son, by His life, death, and resurrection has purchased for us the rewards of eternal life; grant, we beseech thee, that, while meditating on these sacred mysteries of the most holy rosary of the Blessed Virgin Mary, that we may imitate what they contain, and obtain what they promise. Through the same Christ our Lord. Amen.

Mysteries of the Rosary

~ *The Joyful Mysteries* ~

First Joyful Mystery:
THE ANNUNCIATION

And when the angel had come to her, he said, "Hail, full of grace, the Lord is with you" (Lk 1:28).

Our Father, 10 Hail Marys, Glory Be, etc.

FRUIT OF THE MYSTERY: *HUMILITY*

Second Joyful Mystery:
THE VISITATION

Elizabeth was filled with the Holy Spirit and cried out in a loud voice: "Blest are you among women and blest is the fruit of your womb" (Lk 1:41-42).

Our Father, 10 Hail Marys, Glory Be, etc.

FRUIT OF THE MYSTERY:
LOVE OF NEIGHBOR

Third Joyful Mystery:
THE BIRTH OF JESUS

She gave birth to her first-born Son and wrapped Him in swaddling clothes and laid Him in a manger, because there was no room for them in the place where travelers lodged (Lk 2:7).

Our Father, 10 Hail Marys, Glory Be, etc.
FRUIT OF THE MYSTERY: *POVERTY*

Fourth Joyful Mystery:
THE PRESENTATION

When the day came to purify them according to the law of Moses, the couple brought Him up to Jerusalem so that He could be presented to the Lord, for it is written in the law of the Lord, "Every first-born male shall be consecrated to the Lord" (Lk 2:22-23).

Our Father, 10 Hail Marys, Glory Be, etc.
FRUIT OF THE MYSTERY: *OBEDIENCE*

Fifth Joyful Mystery:
FINDING THE CHILD JESUS IN THE TEMPLE

On the third day they came upon Him in the temple sitting in the midst of the teachers, listening to them and asking them questions (Lk 2:46).

Our Father, 10 Hail Marys, Glory Be, etc.

FRUIT OF THE MYSTERY:
JOY IN FINDING JESUS

∼ *The Luminous Mysteries* ∼

First Luminous Mystery:
BAPTISM OF JESUS

And when Jesus was baptized, … the heavens were opened and He saw the Spirit of God descending like a dove, and alighting on Him, and lo, a voice from heaven, saying, "this is My beloved Son, with whom I am well pleased" (Mt 3:16-17).

Our Father, 10 Hail Marys, Glory Be, etc.

FRUIT OF THE MYSTERY:
OPENNESS TO THE HOLY SPIRIT

Second Luminous Mystery:
WEDDING AT CANA

His mother said to the servants, "Do whatever He tells you." Jesus said to them, "Fill the jars with water." And they filled them to the brim (Jn 2:5-7).

Our Father, 10 Hail Marys, Glory Be, etc.

FRUIT OF THE MYSTERY:
TO JESUS THROUGH MARY

Third Luminous Mystery:
PROCLAIMING THE KINGDOM

"And preach as you go, saying, 'The kingdom of heaven is at hand.' Heal the sick, raise the dead, cleanse lepers, cast out demons. You received without pay, give without pay" (Mt 10:7-8).

Our Father, 10 Hail Marys, Glory Be, etc.

FRUIT OF THE MYSTERY:
REPENTANCE AND TRUST IN GOD

Fourth Luminous Mystery:
TRANSFIGURATION

And as He was praying, the appearance of His countenance was altered and His raiment became dazzling white. And a voice came out of the cloud, saying, "This is My Son, My chosen; listen to Him!" (Lk 9:29, 35).

Our Father, 10 Hail Marys, Glory Be, etc.

FRUIT OF THE MYSTERY:
DESIRE FOR HOLINESS

Fifth Luminous Mystery:
INSTITUTION OF THE EUCHARIST

And He took bread, and when He had given thanks He broke it and gave it to them, saying, "This is My body which is given for you." ... And likewise the cup after supper, saying, "This cup which is poured out for you is the new covenant in My blood" (Lk 22:19-20).

Our Father, 10 Hail Marys, Glory Be, etc.

FRUIT OF THE MYSTERY: *ADORATION*

~ *The Sorrowful Mysteries* ~

First Sorrowful Mystery:
THE AGONY IN THE GARDEN

In His anguish, He prayed with all the greater intensity, and His sweat became like drops of blood falling to the ground. Then He rose from prayer and came to His disciples, only to find them asleep, exhausted with grief (Lk 22:44-45).

Our Father, 10 Hail Marys, Glory Be, etc.
FRUIT OF THE MYSTERY:
SORROW FOR SIN

Second Sorrowful Mystery:
THE SCOURGING AT THE PILLAR

Pilate's next move was to take Jesus and have Him scourged (Jn 19:1).

Our Father, 10 Hail Marys, Glory Be, etc.

FRUIT OF THE MYSTERY: *PURITY*

Third Sorrowful Mystery:
CROWNING WITH THORNS

They stripped off His clothes and wrapped Him in a scarlet military cloak. Weaving a crown out of thorns they fixed it on His head, and stuck a reed in His right hand (Mt 27:28-29).

Our Father, 10 Hail Marys, Glory Be, etc.

FRUIT OF THE MYSTERY: *COURAGE*

Fourth Sorrowful Mystery:
CARRYING OF THE CROSS

…[C]arrying the cross by Himself, He went out to what is called the Place of the Skull (in Hebrew, Golgotha) (Jn 19:17).

Our Father, 10 Hail Marys, Glory Be, etc.

FRUIT OF THE MYSTERY: *PATIENCE*

Fifth Sorrowful Mystery:
THE CRUCIFIXION

Jesus uttered a loud cry and said, "Father, into Your hands I commend My spirit." After He said this, He expired (Lk 23:46).

Our Father, 10 Hail Marys, Glory Be, etc.

FRUIT OF THE MYSTERY: *PERSEVERANCE*

~ *The Glorious Mysteries* ~

First Glorious Mystery:
THE RESURRECTION

"You need not be amazed! You are looking for Jesus of Nazareth, the one who was crucified. He has been raised up; He is not here. See the place where they laid Him" (Mk 16:6).

Our Father, 10 Hail Marys, Glory Be, etc.

FRUIT OF THE MYSTERY: *FAITH*

Second Glorious Mystery:
THE ASCENSION

Then, after speaking to them, the Lord Jesus was taken up into heaven and took His seat at God's right hand (Mk 16:19).

Our Father, 10 Hail Marys, Glory Be, etc.

FRUIT OF THE MYSTERY: *HOPE*

Third Glorious Mystery:
DESCENT OF THE HOLY SPIRIT

All were filled with the Holy Spirit. They began to express themselves in foreign tongues and make bold proclamation as the Spirit prompted them (Acts 2:4).

Our Father, 10 Hail Marys, Glory Be, etc.

FRUIT OF THE MYSTERY: *LOVE OF GOD*

Fourth Glorious Mystery:
THE ASSUMPTION

You are the glory of Jerusalem … you are the splendid boast of our people … God is pleased with what you have wrought. May you be blessed by the Lord almighty forever and ever (Jth 15:9-10).

Our Father, 10 Hail Marys, Glory Be, etc

FRUIT OF THE MYSTERY:
GRACE OF A HAPPY DEATH

Fifth Glorious Mystery:
THE CORONATION

A great sign appeared in the sky, a woman clothed with the sun, with the moon under her feet, and on her head a crown of twelve stars (Rev 12:1).

Our Father, 10 Hail Marys, Glory Be, etc

FRUIT OF THE MYSTERY:
TRUST IN MARY'S INTERCESSION

Papal reflections on the Mysteries

The Joyful Mysteries are marked by the joy radiating from the event of the Incarnation. This is clear from the very first mystery, the Annunciation, where Gabriel's greeting to the Virgin of Nazareth is linked to an invitation to messianic joy: "Rejoice, Mary." The whole of salvation … had led up to this greeting. (*Prayed on Mondays and Saturdays, and optional on Sundays during Advent and the Christmas Season.*)

The Luminous Mysteries: Moving on from the infancy and the hidden life in Nazareth to the public life of Jesus, our contemplation brings us to those mysteries which may be called in a special way "mysteries of light." Certainly, the whole mystery of Christ is a mystery of light. He is the "Light of the world" (John 8:12). Yet this truth emerges in a special way during the years of His public life. (*Prayed on Thursdays.*)

The Sorrowful Mysteries: The Gospels give great prominence to the Sorrowful Mysteries of Christ. From the beginning, Christian piety, especially during the Lenten devotion of the Way of the Cross, has focused on the individual moments of the Passion, realizing that here is found the culmination of the revelation of

God's love and the source of our salvation. (*Prayed on Tuesdays and Fridays, and optional on Sundays during Lent.*)

The Glorious Mysteries: "The contemplation of Christ's face cannot stop at the image of the Crucified One. He is the Risen One!" The rosary has always expressed this knowledge born of faith and invited the believer to pass beyond the darkness of the Passion in order to gaze upon Christ's glory in the Resurrection and Ascension. ... Mary herself would be raised to that same glory in the Assumption. (*Prayed on Wednesdays and Sundays.*)

From the Apostolic Letter *The Rosary of the Virgin Mary* (*Rosarium Virginis Mariae*), Pope John Paul II, Oct. 16, 2002.

THE 15 PROMISES OF OUR LADY
made to St. Dominic and Bl. Alan de la Roche

1) To all those who shall recite my rosary devoutly, I promise my special protection and very great graces.

2) Those who shall persevere in the recitation of my rosary shall receive signal graces.

3) The rosary shall be a very powerful armor against hell; it will destroy vice, deliver from sin, and dispel heresy.

4) The rosary will make virtue and good works flourish, and will obtain for souls the most abundant divine mercies; it will draw the hearts of men from the love of the world to the love of God, and will lift them to the desire of eternal things. How many souls shall sanctify themselves by this means!

5) Those who trust themselves to me through the rosary shall not perish.

6) Those who shall recite my rosary devoutly, meditating on its mysteries, shall not be over-whelmed by misfortune. The sinner shall be converted; the just shall grow in grace and become worthy of eternal life.

7) Those truly devoted to my rosary shall not die without the Sacraments of the Church.

8) Those who faithfully recite my rosary shall find during their life and at the hour of their death the light of God, the fullness of his graces, and shall share in the merits of the blessed.

9) I shall deliver very promptly from purgatory the souls devoted to my rosary.

10) The true children of my rosary shall enjoy great glory in heaven.

11) What you ask through my rosary, you shall obtain.

12) Those who propagate my rosary will be aided by me in all their necessities.

13) I have obtained from my Son that all the members of the rosary confraternity shall have as their intercessors, in life and in death, the entire celestial court.

14) Those who recite my rosary faithfully are all my beloved children, the brothers and sisters of Jesus Christ.

15) Devotion to my rosary is a great sign of predestination.

REFERENCES

Dedication:
Blessed Stanislaus Papczynski, *The Crucified Orator,* trans. Thaddaeus Lancton, MIC (Stockbridge, Massachusetts: Marian Press, 2014), 38.

Introduction:
Servant of God Frank Duff, *Virgo Praedicanda* (Dublin, Ireland: Mount Salus Press, 1986), 98.
Blessed James Alberione, *Mary, Mother and Model: Feasts of Mary,* trans. Hilda Calabro, M.A. (Boston, Massachusetts: Daughters of St. Paul, 1958), 200.
St. John Paul II, *Rosarium Virginis Mariae* (October 16, 2002), 17.

January 1: St. John Paul II, Address in Rome (October 8, 1980), as quoted in *John Paul II's Book of Mary,* ed. Margaret R. Bunson (Huntington, Indiana: OSV, 1996), 131.
January 2: Pope Leo XIII, *Audiutricem* (October 5, 1895), 4.
January 3: Blessed Pope Pius IX, as quoted in *The Official Handbook of the Legion of Mary* (Dublin, Ireland: Concilium Legionis Mariae, 2005), 146.
January 4: Venerable Fulton J. Sheen, *The World's First Love: Mary, Mother of God* (San Francisco, California: Ignatius Press, 1996), 209.
January 5: St. John Neumann, as quoted at mostholyrosary.org
January 6: Servant of God (Fr.) Dolindo Ruotolo, *Meditations on the Holy Rosary of Mary,* trans. Giovanna Invitti Ellis (Napoli, Italy, 2006), 36.
January 7: Venerable Pauline Marie Jaricot, as quoted in *Pax Tecum: The Official Newsletter of the Victorian St. Philomena Devotional Center,* Vol. 9. Issue 1 (January 2012), 5.
January 8: Servant of God (Fr.) Patrick Peyton, in "Mary, the Pope, and the American Apostle of the Family Rosary," by Fr. Willy Raymond, CSC, in *Behold Your Mother: Priests Speak about Mary,* ed. Stephen J. Rossetti (Notre Dame, Indiana: Ave Maria Press, 2007), 52.

January 9: Servant of God Pope John Paul I, as quoted in *Humilitas,* English edition, Vol. XXIII, No. 4, December 2012, ed. Ray and Lauretta Seabeck, Mother Teresa, O.C.D., trans. Lori Pieper (Missionary Servants of Pope John Paul I, Beaverton, Oregon).

January 10: St. Louis de Montfort, *The Secret of the Rosary,* trans. Mary Barbour, TOP (Bay Shore, New York: Montfort Publications, 1954), 91.

January 11: Pope Leo XIII, *Adiutricem,* 3.

January 12: St. Alphonsus Liguori, *Hail Holy Queen: An Explanation of the Salve Regina* (Rockford, Illinois: TAN Books, 1995), 225-226.

January 13: Servant of God (Fr.) Dolindo Ruotolo, *Meditations on the Holy Rosary of Mary,* 4.

January 14: St. Louis de Montfort, *True Devotion to the Blessed Virgin* (Bay Shore, New York: Montfort Publications, 1996), 128.

January 15: Blessed Pope Paul VI, *Marialis Cultus* (February 2, 1974), 44.

January 16: St. John Paul II, Beatification Homily (January 21, 1995).

January 17: St. Louis de Montfort, *The Secret of the Rosary,* 9.

January 18: St. John Paul II, *Rosarium Virginis Mariae,* 1.

January 19: Servant of God (Fr.) Joseph Kentenich, *Mary, Our Mother and Educator: An Applied Mariology,* trans. Jonathan Niehaus (Waukesha, Wisconsin: Schoenstatt Sisters, 1987), 11.

January 20: Servant of God (Fr.) Patrick Peyton, as quoted in Jeanne Gosselin Arnold, *A Man of Faith: Father Patrick Peyton, CSC* (Hollywood, California: Family Theater, Inc., 1983), 250.

January 21: Pope Leo XIII, *Fidentem piumque animum* (September 20, 1896), 5.

January 22: St. John Paul II, *Rosarium Virginis Mariae,* 40.

January 23: Blessed William Joseph Chaminade, *Marian Writings,* Vol. 1 (Dayton, Ohio: Marianist Resources Commission, 1980), 58.

January 24: St. Louis de Montfort, *The Secret of the Rosary,* 64.

January 25: St. John Paul II, *Rosarium Virginis Mariae,* 1.

January 26: St. Josemaría Escrivá, *Furrow* (New York: Scepter Press, 1986), 265.

January 27: Blessed George Matulaitis, *De Rosario B.M.V.* (Archivum Generale Congregationis CC. RR. Marianorum. VIII – 154).

January 28: Blessed James Alberione, *Glories and Virtues of Mary,* trans. Hilda Calabro (Boston, Massachusetts: Daughters of St. Paul, 1978), 200.

REFERENCES

January 29: Venerable Fulton J. Sheen, as quoted in Francis Edward Nugent, *Fairest Star Of All: A Little Treasury of Mariology* (Patterson, New Jersey: St. Anthony Guild Press, 1956), 55.

January 30: St. Louis de Montfort, *True Devotion to the Blessed Virgin,* 127-128.

January 31: St. John Bosco, *Forty Dreams of St. John Bosco,* ed. Fr. J. Bacchiarello, SDB (Charlotte, North Carolina: TAN Books, 2012), 110.

February 1: Pope Leo XIII, as quoted in Rev. Charles G. Fehrenbach, C.Ss.R, *Mary Day by Day* (New York: Catholic Book Publishing Co., 1987), 144.

February 2: Venerable Concepción Cabrera de Armida, *Conchita: A Mother's Spiritual Diary,* ed. M. M. Philipon, OP (New York: Alba House, 1978), 171.

February 3: Venerable Fulton J. Sheen, *The World's First Love,* 209.

February 4: St. John Paul II, *Rosarium Virginis Mariae,* 2.

February 5: St. Clement Hofbauer, as quoted in Fehrenbach, *Mary Day by Day,* 145.

February 6: St. John Paul II, Beatification Homily (November 9, 2003).

February 7: Blessed Pope Pius IX, as quoted in Msgr. Joseph A. Cirrincione & Thomas A. Nelson, *The Rosary and the Crisis of Faith* (Rockford, Illinois: TAN Books, 1986), 35.

February 8: Servant of God (Fr.) Patrick Peyton, as quoted in Arnold, *A Man of Faith,* 34.

February 9: Pope Leo XIII, as quoted in Fehrenbach, *Mary Day by Day,* 146.

February 10: Venerable Fulton J. Sheen, *The World's First Love,* 213-214.

February 11: St. Bernadette Soubirous, as quoted in Don Sharkey, *The Woman Shall Conquer: The Story of the Blessed Virgin in the Modern World* (Milwaukee: Bruce Publishing Company, 1952), 56.

February 12: St. Maximilian Kolbe, *Aim Higher,* trans. Fr. Dominic Wisz, OFM, Conv., (Libertyville, Illinois: Marytown Press, 2007), 96-97.

February 13: Pope Leo XIII, *Adiutricem,* 24.

February 14: Servant of God (Fr.) Patrick Peyton, in "Mary, the Pope, and the American Apostle of the Family Rosary," by Fr. Willy Raymond, CSC in *Behold Your Mother: Priests Speak about Mary.* (ed.). Stephen J. Rossetti (Notre Dame, Indiana: Ave Maria Press, 2007), 53.

February 15: Blessed Michael Sopocko, *The Mercy of God in His Works: Vol. IV*, trans. R. Batchelor (Hereford: Marian Apostolate, 1972), 86.

February 16: St. Padre Pio, as quoted in Liz Kelly, *The Rosary: A Path to Prayer* (Chicago, Illinois: Loyola Press, 2004), 86.

February 17: Servant of God (Fr.) John Hardon, *Our Lady of the Rosary: A Marian Retreat,* as quoted at therealpresence.org

February 18: St. Louis de Montfort, *The Secret of the Rosary,* 9.

February 19: Blessed Francisco Marto, as quoted in Servant of God Lúcia Dos Santos, *Fatima in Lucia's Own Words* (Fatima, Portugal: Secretariado Dos Pastorinhos, 2011), 143.

February 20: Servant of God Lúcia Dos Santos, *Fatima in Lucia's Own Words* (Fatima, Portugal: Secretariado Dos Pastorinhos, 2011), 50.

February 21: Servant of God (Fr.) Patrick Peyton, as quoted in Arnold, *A Man of Faith,* 250.

February 22: St. John Paul II, Address at Fatima (May 13, 1982), as quoted in *John Paul II's Book of Mary,* ed. Margaret R. Bunson (Huntington, Indiana: OSV, 1996), 129.

February 23: Pope Leo XIII, as quoted in Cirrincione, *The Rosary and the Crisis of Faith,* 34-35.

February 24: St. John Paul II, *Rosarium Virginis Mariae,* 3.

February 25: St. John Paul II, Beatification Homily (October 3, 2004).

February 26: Pope Pius XI, *Ingravescentibus Malis* (September 29, 1937), 29.

February 27: St. Josemaría Escrivá, *Holy Rosary* (New York: Scepter Press, 2003), 9.

February 28: St. Louis de Montfort, *The Secret of the Rosary,* 9.

February 29: St. Pope John XXIII, as quoted in Servant of God (Fr.) Patrick Peyton, *All For Her* (Hollywood, California: Family Theater Productions, 1973), 189.

March 1: Servant of God (Fr.) Patrick Peyton, as quoted in Arnold, *A Man of Faith,* 48.

March 2: Blessed Pope Pius IX, as quoted in Sharkey, *The Woman Shall Conquer,* 246.

March 3: Venerable Fulton J. Sheen, *The World's First Love: Mary,* 210.

March 4: St. John Paul II, Address in Rome (October 8, 1980), as quoted in *John Paul II's Book of Mary,* ed. Margaret R. Bunson (Huntington, Indiana: OSV, 1996), 131-132.

March 5: St. Josemaría Escrivá, *The Way,* no. 558, p.117, as quoted in Jason Evert, *Purity 365: Daily Reflections on True Love* (Cincinnati, Ohio: Servant Books, 2009), 105.

March 6: Pope Leo XIII, *Adiutricem,* 25.

March 7: St. John Paul II, *Rosarium Virginis Mariae,* 3.

March 8: Venerable Fulton J. Sheen, *The World's First Love,* 214-215.

March 9: Blessed Pope Paul VI, *Marialis Cultus,* 47.

REFERENCES

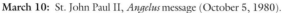

March 10: St. John Paul II, *Angelus* message (October 5, 1980).

March 11: Servant of God (Fr.) Dolindo Ruotolo, *Meditations on the Holy Rosary of Mary*, 35.

March 12: Servant of God (Fr.) Patrick Peyton, as quoted in Arnold, *A Man of Faith,* 63.

March 13: Venerable Pope Pius XII, as quoted in Arnold, *A Man of Faith,* 99.

March 14: St. Pope John XXIII, as quoted in Arnold, *A Man of Faith,* 133.

March 15: St. Louise de Marillac, as quoted in Rory Michael Fox, *Saints, Popes and Blesseds Speak on the Rosary* [E-reader version], 2012.

March 16: Pope Francis, Address at the Vigil of Pentecost with the Ecclesial Movements, (May 18, 2013).

March 17: Blessed Pope Paul VI, *Marialis Cultus,* 46.

March 18: St. John Paul II, *Rosarium Virginis Mariae,* 4.

March 19: St. Louis de Montfort, *The Secret of the Rosary,* 16.

March 20: Pope Benedict XVI, Canonization Homily (October 23, 2005).

March 21: Servant of God (Fr.) Dolindo Ruotolo, *Meditations on the Holy Rosary of Mary*, 5.

March 22: St. Josemaría Escrivá, *Holy Rosary,* 11.

March 23: Blessed Bartolo Longo, as quoted in Ann M. Brown, *Apostle of the Rosary: Blessed Bartolo Longo* (New Hope, Kentucky: New Hope Publications, 2004), 43.

March 24: Blessed Pope Paul VI, *"Recurrens Mensis October,"* (October 7, 1969).

March 25: St. John Paul II, *Rosarium Virginis Mariae,* 33.

March 26: Servant of God (Fr.) Patrick Peyton, as quoted in Arnold, *A Man of Faith,* 250.

March 27: Pope Leo XIII, *Adiutricem,* 26.

March 28: Pope Pius XI, as quoted in Fehrenbach, *Mary Day by Day,* 148.

March 29: St. Louis de Montfort, *The Secret of the Rosary,* 93.

March 30: St. John Paul II, *Rosarium Virginis Mariae,* 5.

March 31: St. Louis de Montfort, *The Secret of the Rosary,* 12.

April 1: Servant of God Pope John Paul I, as quoted in *Humilitas,* English Edition, Vol. XXIII, No. 4 (December 2012).

April 2: Pope Leo XIII, *Adiutricem,* 27.

April 3: Venerable Fulton J. Sheen, *The World's First Love,* 210.

April 4: St. Pope John XXIII, as quoted in Fehrenbach, *Mary Day by Day,* 148.

April 5: St. Alphonsus Liguori, *The Glories of Mary* (Charlotte, North Carolina: TAN Books, 2012), 545.

April 6: Servant of God (Fr.) Patrick Peyton, as quoted in Arnold, *A Man of Faith,* 250.

April 7: St. Louis de Montfort, *The Secret of the Rosary,* 17-18.

April 8: St. John Paul II, *Rosarium Virginis Mariae,* 6.

April 9: Blessed Bartolo Longo, as quoted in Brown, *Apostle of the Rosary,* 53.

April 10: Blessed Pope Paul VI, *Marialis Cultus,* 48.

April 11: St. John Paul II, *Rosarium Virginis Mariae,* 25.

April 12: Venerable Pauline Jaricot, as quoted in Mary Fabyan Windeatt, *Pauline Jaricot* (Rockford, Illinois: TAN, 1993), 68.

April 13: St. Alphonsus Liguori, *Hail Holy Queen,* 226.

April 14: St. John Paul II, *Angelus* message (October 1, 1995).

April 15: Pope Francis, *Angelus* message (October 6, 2013).

April 16: St. Louis de Montfort, *The Secret of the Rosary,* 98.

April 17: St. John Paul II, *Rosarium Virginis Mariae,* 7.

April 18: St. Louis de Montfort, *The Secret of the Rosary,* 26.

April 19: Servant of God (Fr.) Dolindo Ruotolo, *Meditations on the Holy Rosary of Mary,* 36.

April 20: Servant of God Frank Duff, *Virgo Praedicanda,* 102.

April 21: Pope Pius XI, *Ingravescentibus Malis,* 15.

April 22: Blessed Bartolo Longo, as quoted in St. John Paul II, *Rosarium Virginis Mariae,* 15.

April 23: Venerable María del Carmen González-Valerio, as quoted in Ann Ball, *Young Faces of Holiness* (Huntington, Indiana: OSV, 2004), 107.

April 24: Servant of God Lúcia Dos Santos, *'Calls' from the Message of Fatima* (Fatima, Portugal: Secretariado dos Pastorinhos, 2000), 134.

April 25: Blessed John Henry Newman, *Mary, the Second Eve* (Rockford, Illinois: TAN, 1982), 36.

April 26: St. John Paul II, *Rosarium Virginis Mariae,* 14.

April 27: Pope Leo XIII, *Adiutricem,* 27.

April 28: St. Louis de Montfort, *The Secret of the Rosary,* 61.

April 29: Servant of God (Fr.) Patrick Peyton, as quoted in Arnold, *A Man of Faith,* 268.

April 30: St. Josemaría Escrivá, *Holy Rosary,* 12.

REFERENCES

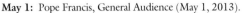

May 1: Pope Francis, General Audience (May 1, 2013).

May 2: Servant of God Lúcia Dos Santos, *Fatima in Lucia's Own Words: Volume II* (Fatima, Portugal: Secretariado dos Pastorinhos, 2006), 106.

May 3: Venerable Fulton J. Sheen, *The World's First Love,* 211.

May 4: Pope Benedict XVI, Papal Address (June 11, 2011).

May 5: St. John Paul II, Beatification Homily (May 4, 1997).

May 6: Pope Francis, Homily (August 15, 2013).

May 7: Servant of God (Fr.) Dolindo Ruotolo, *Meditations on the Holy Rosary of Mary,* 5.

May 8: Venerable Pope Pius XII, as quoted in Cirrincione, *The Rosary and the Crisis of Faith,* 33.

May 9: St. Louis de Montfort, *The Secret of the Rosary,* 27.

May 10: St. John Paul II, *Rosarium Virginis Mariae,* 41.

May 11: Servant of God (Fr.) John A. Hardon, *The Rosary: A Prayer for all Times,* as quoted at therealpresence.org.

May 12: Pope Leo XIII, *Augustissimae Virginia Mariae* (September 12, 1897), 8.

May 13: Our Lady of Fatima, as quoted in Sharkey, *The Woman Shall Conquer,* 243.

May 14: St. John Paul II, Address at Fatima (May 13, 1982), as quoted in *John Paul II's Book of Mary,* ed. Margaret R. Bunson (Huntington, Indiana: OSV, 1996), 128-129.

May 15: Pope Pius XI, *Ingravescentibus Malis,* 9.

May 16: Servant of God (Fr.) Joseph Kententich, *The Marian Person,* trans. Jonathan Niehaus (Waukesha, Wisconsin: Schoenstatt Fathers, 2007), 37.

May 17: St. Alphonsus Liguori, *Hail Holy Queen,* 226.

May 18: Servant of God Lúcia Dos Santos, *Letter to Mother Martins,* as quoted in Cirrincione, *The Rosary and the Crisis of Faith,* 16.

May 19: Servant of God (Fr.) Patrick Peyton, *All For Her* (Hollywood, California: Family Theater Productions, 1973), 1.

May 20: St. Louis de Montfort, *The Secret of the Rosary,* 27.

May 21: Venerable Nelson Baker, as quoted in Richard Gribble, CSC, "Father Nelson Baker and the Blessed Virgin Mary: A Lifetime of Devotion," in Marian Studies. Vol.LXII (2011): 110-111.

May 22: Venerable Faustino Perez-Manglano, as quoted in Joan Carroll Cruz, *Saintly Youth of Modern Times* (Huntington, Indiana: OSV, 2006), 82.

May 23: St. John Paul II, *Rosarium Virginis Mariae,* 41

May 24: St. Pope John XXIII, *Grata Recordatio* (September 26, 1959), 2.

May 25: St. Francis de Sales, as quoted in *St. Francis de Sales and Mary,* ed. Antony Kolencherry, MSFS, (Bangalore: SFS Publications, 1988), 58.

May 26: Blessed James Alberione, *Glories and Virtues of Mary,* 52.

May 27: St. Eugène de Mazenod, as quoted at oblatesusa.org.

May 28: St. John Paul II, General Audience (October 8, 1980).

May 29: Blessed Pope Paul VI, *Mense Maio* (April 29, 1965), 14.

May 30: St. Louis de Montfort, *The Secret of the Rosary,* 28.

May 31: Venerable Teresa of Jesus Quevedo, as quoted in Sr. Mary Pierre, R.S.M., *Mary Was Her Life: The Story of a Nun* (New York: Benziger Brothers, Inc., 1960), 9.

June 1: St. John Paul II, *Rosarium Virginis Mariae,* 5.

June 2: Venerable Fulton J. Sheen, *The World's First Love,* 211.

June 3: St. Pope John XXIII, as quoted in Andrew J. Gerakas, *The Rosary and Devotion to Mary* (Boston, Massachusetts: St. Paul Books & Media, 1992), 23.

June 4: Blessed Teresa of Calcutta, *Heart of Joy* (Ann Arbor, Michigan: Servant Books, 1987), 19.

June 5: Pope Urban IV, as quoted in Pope Leo XIII, *Supremi Apostolatus Officio* (September 1, 1883), 5.

June 6: St. Louis de Montfort, *The Secret of the Rosary,* 29.

June 7: Servant of God (Fr.) Dolindo Ruotolo, *Meditations on the Holy Rosary of Mary,* 41.

June 8: St. Louis de Montfort, *The Secret of the Rosary,* 85.

June 9: St. John Paul II, *Rosarium Virginis Mariae,* 25.

June 10: Pope Leo XIII, *Diuturni Temporis* (September 5, 1898), 5-6.

June 11: St. Josemaría Escrivá, *Furrow,* 186.

June 12: Pope Pius XI, as quoted in Fehrenbach, *Mary Day by Day,* 149.

June 13: Pope Adrian VI, as quoted in Sr. Patricia Proctor, OSC, *101 Inspirational Stories on the Rosary* (Spokane, Washington: Franciscan Monastery, 2003), 180.

June 14: Blessed Pope Paul VI, *Marialis Cultus,* 54.

June 15: St. Pope Pius V, as quoted in David Supple, *Virgin Wholly Marvelous* (Cambridge, Massachusetts: Ravengate, 1991), 131.

REFERENCES

June 16: St. Alphonsus Liguori, *The Glories of Mary* (Charlotte, North Carolina: TAN Books, 2012), 545.

June 17: Blessed Bartolo Longo, as quoted in Brown, *Apostle of the Rosary*, 53.

June 18: St. Louis de Montfort, *The Secret of the Rosary*, 58.

June 19: Servant of God (Fr.) Joseph Kentenich, *Marian Instrument Piety* (Waukesha, Wisconsin: Schoenstatt Center, 1992), 116.

June 20: Servant of God (Fr.) Patrick Peyton, *Family Prayer* (New York: Benziger Bros., Inc., 1964), 13.

June 21: Servant of God (Fr.) Walter Ciszek, *With God in Russia* (San Francisco, California: Ignatius Press, 1997), 418.

June 22: Blessed James Alberione, *Glories and Virtues of Mary*, 37.

June 23: St. John Paul II, General Audience (October 1, 2003).

June 24: Blessed Pope Paul VI, *Christi Matri* (September 15, 1966), 9.

June 25: Pope Leo XIII, as quoted in Fehrenbach, *Mary Day by Day*, 150.

June 26: St. Josemaría Escrivá, *Furrow*, 186-187.

June 27: Pope Gregory XII, as quoted in Proctor, *101 Inspirational Stories on the Rosary*, 102.

June 28: St. Louis de Montfort, as quoted in Fehrenbach, *Mary Day by Day*, 149.

June 29: Pope St. John XXIII, *"Radio Message for the Coronation of Our Lady of the Rosary of La Coruña, Spain"* (September 11, 1960), trans. Ileana E. Salazar, M.A.

June 30: Servant of God (Fr.) Joseph Kentenich, *Mary, Our Mother and Educator: An Applied Mariology*, trans. Jonathan Niehaus (Waukesha, Wisconsin: Schoenstatt Sisters, 1987), 11.

July 1: St. John Paul II, Beatification Homily (May 9, 2001).

July 2: Servant of God Lúcia Dos Santos, *Letter to Mother Martins*, as quoted in Cirrincione, *The Rosary and the Crisis of Faith*, 16.

July 3: Venerable Fulton J. Sheen, *The World's First Love*, 212.

July 4: Pope Pius XI, as quoted in Cirrincione, *The Rosary and the Crisis of Faith*, 33.

July 5: Blessed Pier Giorgio Frassati, as quoted in Maria Di Lorenzo, *Blessed Pier Giorgio Frassati: An Ordinary Christian* (Boston, Massachusetts: Pauline Books, 2004), 53.

July 6: St. John Paul II, Address in Rome (October 8, 1980), as quoted in *John Paul*

237

II's Book of Mary, ed. Margaret R. Bunson (Huntington, Indiana: OSV, 1996), 131.

July 7: Blessed Pope Paul VI, as quoted in Cirrincione, *The Rosary and the Crisis of Faith*, 32.

July 8: St. Louis de Montfort, *The Secret of the Rosary*, 62.

July 9: Servant of God Frank Duff, *Virgo Praedicanda*, 100.

July 10: Servant of God (Fr.) John A. Hardon, *The Rosary: A Prayer for all Times*, as quoted at therealpresence.org.

July 11: Venerable Pope Pius XII, *Mediator Dei*, 173-174.

July 12: Servant of God (Fr.) Joseph Kentenich, *Talk by Fr. Joseph Kentenich in the Church at Ennabeuren, Germany* (May 3, 1945). Courtesy of Schoenstatt Sisters, Waukesha, Wisconsin.

July 13: Pope Pius XI, *Ingravescentibus Malis*, 28.

July 14: St. John Paul II, *Rosarium Virginis Mariae*, 15.

July 15: St. Josemaría Escrivá, *Christ is Passing By* (Manila: Sinag-Tala, 1973), 325.

July 16: Servant of God (Fr.) Joseph Kentenich, *Mary, Our Mother and Educator*, 153.

July 17: Pope Leo XIII, Apostolic Letter *Salutaris Ille Spiritus* (December 24, 1883), 2.

July 18: Servant of God (Fr.) Patrick Peyton, as quoted in Arnold, *A Man of Faith*, 27.

July 19: Pope Pius XI, *Ingravescentibus Malis*, 12.

July 20: St. John Vianney, *Thoughts of the Curé D'Ars* (Rockford, Illinois: TAN Books, 1984), 60.

July 21: Blessed Teresa of Calcutta, as quoted in Susan Conroy, *Praying in the Presence of Our Lord with Mother Teresa* (Huntington, Indiana: OSV, 2005), 70.

July 22: St. Alphonsus Liguori, *The Glories of Mary*, 546.

July 23: St. Louis de Montfort, *The Secret of the Rosary*, 67.

July 24: St. John Paul II, *Rosarium Virginis Mariae*, 26.

July 25: Servant of God Dorothy Day, as quoted in David Scott, *Praying in the Presence of Our Lord with Dorothy Day* (Huntington, Indiana: OSV, 2002), 38-39.

July 26: Blessed Bartolo Longo, as quoted in Rory Michael Fox, *Saints, Popes and Blesseds Speak on the Rosary* [E-reader version], 2012.

July 27: Servant of God (Fr.) Joseph Kentenich, *Talk by Fr. Joseph Kentenich in the Church at Ennabeuren, Germany* (May 3, 1945). Courtesy of Schoenstatt Sisters, Waukesha, Wisconsin.

REFERENCES

July 28: Blessed Pope Pius IX, as quoted in Patrick J. Peyton, *The Ear of God* (Garden City, New York: Doubleday, 1951), 107.

July 29: Servant of God Lúcia Dos Santos, *'Calls' from the Message of Fatima* (Fatima, Portugal: Secretariado dos Pastorinhos, 2000), 271.

July 30: Pope Pius XI, *Inclytam ac perillustrem* (Letter to R.P. Gillet, Master General of the Dominicans, March 6, 1934), as quoted in *Our Lady: Papal Teachings* (Boston, Massachusetts: Daughters of St. Paul, 1961), 228.

July 31: St. Francis de Sales, as quoted in Kolencherry, *St. Francis de Sales and Mary,* 68.

August 1: St. Alphonsus Liguori, *Hail Holy Queen,* 226.

August 2: St. Louis de Montfort, *The Secret of the Rosary,* 71.

August 3: Blessed Pope Paul VI, as quoted in Fehrenbach, *Mary Day by Day,* 150.

August 4: St. John Vianney, *Thoughts of the Cure D'Ars.* (Charlotte, North Carolina: TAN Books, 1984), 59.

August 5: Venerable Fulton J. Sheen, *The World's First Love,* 212.

August 6: Servant of God (Fr.) Patrick Peyton, *All For Her,* 6.

August 7: St. John Paul II, *Rosarium Virginis Mariae,* 26.

August 8: Pope Leo XIII, *Adiutricem,* 12.

August 9: Pope Leo XIII, *Supremi Apostolatus Officio,* 7.

August 10: Venerable Pope Pius XII, *Ingruentium Malorum* (September 15, 1951), 15.

August 11: St. Louis de Montfort, *The Secret of the Rosary,* 84-85.

August 12: St. Jane Frances de Chantal, as quoted in Kolencherry, *St. Francis de Sales and Mary,* 15.

August 13: Servant of God (Fr.) Dolindo Ruotolo, *Meditations on the Holy Rosary of Mary,* 41.

August 14: St. Maximilian Kolbe, *Aim Higher,* 97.

August 15: Blessed Dina Bélanger, *The Autobiography of Dina Bélanger* (Québec, Canada: Religious of Jesus and Mary, 1997), 146.

August 16: St. John Paul II in *L'Osservatore Romano* (October 1983), as quoted in *John Paul II's Book of Mary,* ed. Margaret R. Bunson (Huntington, Indiana: OSV, 1996), 128.

August 17: Pope Pius XI, *Ingravescentibus Malis,* 16.

August 18: St. Josemaría Escrivá, *Friends of God* (New York: Scepter, 1981), 450.

August 19: Pope Leo XIII, *Diuturni Temporis* (September 5, 1898), 3.

August 20: St. Louis de Montfort, *The Secret of the Rosary*, 80-81.

August 21: St. Pope Pius X, as quoted in Cirrincione, *The Rosary and the Crisis of Faith*, 34.

August 22: Blessed Bartolo Longo, as quoted in Brown, *Apostle of the Rosary*, 51.

August 23: St. John Paul II, *Rosarium Virginis Mariae*, 38

August 24: Servant of God Frank Duff, *Virgo Praedicanda*, 101.

August 25: Blessed James Alberione, *Glories and Virtues of Mary*, 52.

August 26: Servant of God (Fr.) Joseph Kentenich, *Talk by Fr. Joseph Kentenich in the Church at Ennabeuren, Germany* (May 3, 1945). Courtesy of Schoenstatt Sisters, Waukesha, Wisconsin.

August 27: Blessed James Alberione, *Mary, Queen of Apostles* (Boston, Massachusetts: Daughters of St. Paul, 1976), 179.

August 28: Pope Pius XI, *Ingravescentibus Malis*, 23.

August 29: Pope Leo XIII, *Fidentem piumque animum*, 3.

August 30: Pope Benedict XVI, General Audience (October 8, 2008).

August 31: Pope Leo XIII, *Fidentem piumque animum*, 2.

September 1: Blessed Alan de la Roche, as quoted in Fehrenbach, *Mary Day by Day*, 147.

September 2: St. John Paul II, *Rosarium Virginis Mariae*, 39.

September 3: Venerable Fulton J. Sheen, *The World's First Love*, 213.

September 4: St. Alphonsus Liguori, *The Glories of Mary*, 546.

September 5: Blessed Teresa of Calcutta, *From a Letter to Father Lawrence T. Picachy, S.J.* (February 13, 1963), as quoted in Fr. Benedict J. Groeschel, C.F.R., *The Rosary: Chain of Hope* (San Francisco, California: Ignatius Press, 2003), 16.

September 6: St. Pope John XXIII, as quoted in Cirrincione, *The Rosary and the Crisis of Faith*, 32.

September 7: Pope Leo XIII, *Fidentem piumque animum*, 5.

September 8: St. John Paul II, Address in Manila (February 17, 1981), as quoted in *John Paul II's Book of Mary*, ed. Margaret R. Bunson (Huntington, Indiana: OSV, 1996), 127.

September 9: St. Louis de Montfort, *The Secret of the Rosary*, 86.

September 10: Servant of God (Fr.) Joseph Kentenich, *Talk by Fr. Joseph Kentenich in the Church at Ennabeuren, Germany* (May 3, 1945). Courtesy of Schoenstatt Sisters, Waukesha, Wisconsin.

REFERENCES

September 11: St. John Paul II, *Angelus* message (September 30, 2001).

September 12: Pope Leo XIII, *Augustissimae Virginia Mariae*, 9.

September 13: Blessed Bartolo Longo, as quoted in St. John Paul II, Beatification Homily (October 26, 1980).

September 14: Venerable Fulton J. Sheen, *The World's First Love*, 213.

September 15: Pope Leo XIII, *Lucunda Semper Expectatione* (September 8, 1894), 2.

September 16: St. Josemaría Escrivá, *Furrow*, 186.

September 17: St. Pope Pius X, as quoted at marypage.org

September 18: Blessed Charles de Foucauld, as quoted in Dom Antoine Marie, OSB. *Spiritual Newsletter* (Abbey of Saint-Joseph de Clairval, France: January 25, 2006).

September 19: Venerable Pope Pius XII, as quoted in Cirrincione , *The Rosary and the Crisis of Faith*, 33.

September 20: St. Louis de Montfort, *The Secret of the Rosary*, 91.

September 21: St. John Paul II, *Rosarium Virginis Mariae*, 40.

September 22: Servant of God Frank Duff, *Virgo Praedicanda*, 101.

September 23: St. Padre Pio, as quoted by St. John Paul II in Fr. Robert J. Fox, *First Saturdays for the Triumph of the Immaculate Heart* (Minnesota: Fatima Family Apostolate, 2000), 39.

September 24: St. John Paul II, *Rosarium Virginis Mariae*, 41.

September 25: Pope Gregory XVI, as quoted at marypage.org

September 26: St. Josemaría Escrivá, *Holy Rosary*, 14.

September 27: St. Clement Hofbauer, as quoted in Servant of God (Fr.) Joseph Kentenich, *Marian Instrument Piety* (Waukesha, Wisconsin: Schoenstatt Center, 1992), 119.

September 28: St. John Paul II, Canonization Homily (July 3, 1988).

September 29: Pope Leo XIII, *Augustissimae Virginia Mariae*, 10.

September 30: St. John Paul II, *Rosarium Virginis Mariae*, 42.

October 1: St. Thérèse of Lisieux, as quoted in Romanus Cessario, O.P., *Perpetual Angelus: As the Saints Pray the Rosary* (Staten Island, New York: Alba House, 1995), 136.

October 2: St. Faustina Kowalska, *Diary: Divine Mercy in My Soul* (Stockbridge, Massachusetts: Marian Helpers, 2002), no. 314.

October 3: Blessed Columba Marmion, *The Mysteries of the Rosary* (Veritas Spendor Publications, 2012), 12.

October 4: Pope Francis, Homily for Family Day (October 27, 2013).

October 5: Blessed Bartolo Longo, *Supplication to the Queen of the Holy Rosary,* as quoted in St. John Paul II, *Rosarium Virginis Mariae,* 43.

October 6: Venerable Fulton J. Sheen, *The World's First Love,* 214.

October 7: Pope Benedict XVI, *Angelus* message (October 1, 2006).

October 8: St. John Paul II, *Familiaris Consortio* (November 22, 1981), 61.

October 9: Blessed John Henry Newman, *Meditation For the Feast of the Holy Rosary* (October 5, 1879), as quoted in *L'Osservatore Romano* (February 5, 2003), 10.

October 10: Pope Leo XIII, *Lucunda Semper Expectatione,* 7.

October 11: St. Pope John XXIII, as quoted in Francis Beauchesne Thornton, *This is the Rosary* (New York: Hawthorn Books, 1961), 10.

October 12: St. Louis de Montfort, *True Devotion to the Blessed Virgin,* 25-26.

October 13: Our Lady of Fatima, as quoted in Sharkey, *The Woman Shall Conquer,* 243.

October 14: St. John Paul II, *In Response to questions about the Third Secret whilst speaking in Fulda, Germany* (1980), as quoted in *Magnificat,* Vol. 15, No. 8 (October 2013), 308.

October 15: Blessed Alberto Marvelli, as quoted in St. John Paul II in *Homily of Beatification of Alberto Marvelli* (Esplanade of Montorso, Loreto: September 5, 2004), vatican.va

October 16: Pope Leo XIII, *Laetitiae Sanctae* (September 8, 1893), 3.

October 17: Pope Pius XI, *Ingravescentibus Malis,* 22.

October 18: St. Josemaría Escrivá, *Friends of God* (New York: Scepter, 1981), 461.

October 19: Pope Benedict XV, as quoted in Cirrincione, *The Rosary and the Crisis of Faith,* 34.

October 20: St. Paul of the Cross, as quoted in Catherine Moran, *Praying the Rosary with the Saints* [E-reader version], 2013.

October 21: St. Louis de Montfort, *The Secret of the Rosary,* 13.

October 22: St. John Paul II, *Angelus* message *(Insegnamenti di Giovanni Paolo II,* I (1978): 75-76.

October 23: Blessed Timothy Giaccardo, as quoted in *Spiritual Advice from the Saints: 365 Days of Inspiration.* Compiled by Daughters of St. Paul (Boston, Massachusetts: Pauline Books & Media, 2004), entry for October 7.

October 24: St. Anthony Mary Claret, as quoted at: www.rosarymission.org

October 25: Blessed Francis Xavier Seelos, *Seelos Center News,* Vol. XLVI, No.5. May 2007.

October 26: Pope Benedict XVI, *Angeles* message (October 3, 2010)

October 27: Blessed Pope Paul VI, *Christi Matri,* 10.

October 28: St. Louis de Montfort, *The Secret of the Rosary,* 96.

October 29: Servant of God (Fr.) John A. Hardon, *The Rosary: A Prayer for all Times,* as quoted at: www.therealpresence.org

October 30: Pope Leo XIII, *Laetitiae Sanctae,* 18.

October 31: Blessed Bartolo Longo, as quoted at marypage.org

November 1: St. Louis de Montfort, *The Secret of the Rosary,* 64-65.

November 2: St. Alphonsus de Liguori, as quoted in Catherine Moran, *Praying the Rosary with the Saints* [E-reader version], 2013.

November 3: Servant of God Elisabeth Leseur, *The Secret Diary of Elisabeth Leseur: The Woman Whose Goodness Changed Her Husband from Atheist to Priest* (Manchester, New Hampshire: Sophia Institute Press, 2002), 223.

November 4: St. John Vianney, *The Sermons of the Curé of Ars,* trans. Una Morrissy (Charlotte, North Carolina: TAN Books, 1995), 215.

November 5: St. John Paul II, *Address at Nuaro, Italy* (October 19, 1985), as quoted in *John Paul II's Book of Mary,* ed. Margaret R. Bunson (Huntington, Indiana: OSV, 1996), 130.

November 6: Pope Leo XIII, *Magnae Dei Matris* (September 8, 1892), 7.

November 7: Servant of God Frank Duff, *Virgo Praedicanda,* 95.

November 8: St. Pope John XXIII, as quoted in Arnold, *A Man of Faith,* 175.

November 9: St. Louis de Montfort, *The Secret of the Rosary,* 96.

November 10: St. John Paul II, Message to the Bishop of Leiria-Fatima (October 1, 1997).

November 11: Blessed Pope Paul VI, *Marialis Cultus,* 52.

November 12: Servant of God Frank Duff, *Virgo Praedicanda,* 97.

November 13: St. Alphonsus Liguori, *Hail Holy Queen,* 35.

November 14: St. John Paul II, *Rosarium Virginis Mariae,* 43.

November 15: Servant of God Lúcia Dos Santos, *Letter to Mother Martins,* as quoted in Cirrincione, *The Rosary and the Crisis of Faith,* 15.

November 16: Servant of God Rafael (Cardinal) Merry del Val, as quoted in Rev. Jerome Dal-gal, *The Spiritual Life of Cardinal Merry del Val* (New York: Benziger Bros, Inc., 1959), 113-114.

November 17: St. Louis de Montfort, *The Secret of the Rosary*, 97.

November 18: Pope Leo XIII, *Magnae Dei Matris*, 18.

November 19: Servant of God Frank Duff, *Virgo Praedicanda*, 101-102.

November 20: St. Pope John XXIII, as quoted in Peyton, *All For Her*, 189.

November 21: Pope Pius XI, as quoted in Cirrincione, *The Rosary and the Crisis of Faith*, 33.

November 22: Servant of God (Fr.) Joseph Kentenich, *Mary, Our Mother and Educator*, 11.

November 23: St. Josemaría Escrivá, *Holy Rosary*, 15.

November 24: St. Francis de Sales, as quoted in Kolencherry, *St. Francis de Sales and Mary*, 68.

November 25: St. John Paul II, Beatification Homily (October 21, 2001).

November 26: Blessed James Alberione, *Glories and Virtues of Mary*, 37.

November 27: Blessed James Alberione, *Glories and Virtues of Mary*, 52.

November 28: Blessed Bartolo Longo, as quoted in Brown, *Apostle of the Rosary*, 27.

November 29: St. John Paul II, *Angelus* message (October 6, 1991).

November 30: Servant of God Lúcia Dos Santos, as quoted in Rory Michael Fox, *Saints, Popes and Blesseds Speak on the Rosary* [E-reader version], 2012.

December 1: Servant of God Pope John Paul I, as quoted in *Humilitas*, English Edition, Vol. XXIII, No. 4 (December, 2012).

December 2: Blessed Pope Paul VI, as quoted in Arnold, *A Man of Faith*, 202.

December 3: Pope Benedict XV, *Di altissimo pregio* (September 18, 1915)

December 4: St. Louis de Montfort, *The Secret of the Rosary*, 98.

December 5: Venerable Faustino Perez-Manglano, as quoted in Ball, *Young Faces of Holiness*, 62.

December 6: Pope Benedict XVI, *Angelus* message (October 7, 2012).

December 7: Pope Leo XIII, *Magnae Dei Matris*, 29.

December 8: St. Eugène de Mazenod, *CC&RR, Constitutions*, 36.

December 9: Servant of God Lúcia Dos Santos, *'Calls' from the Message of Fatima* (Fatima, Portugal: Secretariado dos Pastorinhos, 2000), 132.

December 10: St. Louis de Montfort, *True Devotion to the Blessed Virgin*, 180.

December 11: St. John Paul II, *Angelus* message (March 23, 2003).

December 12: Blessed James Alberione, *Mary Leads Us to Jesus: The Marian Spirituality of Blessed James Alberione, SSP*, ed. Marianne Lorraine Trouvé, FSP (Boston, Massachusetts: Pauline Books & Media, 2004), 78.

December 13: Venerable Teresa of Jesus Quevedo, as quoted in Pierre, *Mary Was Her Life*, 184.

December 14: Pope Leo XIII, *Octobri Mense*, 7.

December 15: Servant of God Frank Duff, *Virgo Praedicanda*, 94.

December 16: Pope Benedict XVI, Meditation from the *Pastoral Visit to Shrine of Pompeii* (October 19, 2008).

December 17: Venerable Fulton J. Sheen, *The World's First Love*, 208.

December 18: Servant of God (Fr.) Patrick Peyton, as quoted in Arnold, *A Man of Faith*, 295.

December 19: Pope Leo XIII, *Vi é ben noto*, (September 20, 1897), 3.

December 20: St. John Paul II, *Rosarium Virginis Mariae*, 43.

December 21: St. Luigi Orione, *On The Way With Don Orione* (Staten Island, New York: Alba House, 1974), 150.

December 22: Venerable Fulton J. Sheen, *The World's First Love: Mary*, 216.

December 23: Blessed James Alberione, *Mary, Mother and Model*, 200.

December 24: Blessed Columba Marmion, *The Mysteries of the Rosary*, trans. Paul A. Böer, Sr. [Veritatis Splendor Publications: E-Reader Version], 2012.

December 25: Venerable Fulton J. Sheen, *The World's First Love: Mary*, 211.

December 26: Venerable Solanus Casey, as quoted in Leo Wollenweber, OFM, Cap., *Meet Solanus Casey: Spiritual Counselor and Wonder Worker* (Cincinnati, Ohio: Servant Books, 2002), 95.

December 27: Servant of God (Fr.) Dolindo Ruotolo, *Meditations on the Holy Rosary of Mary*, 3.

December 28: Blessed Bartolo Longo, as quoted in Brown, *Apostle of the Rosary*, 55.

December 29: Pope Francis, Video Message on the Occasion of the Prayer Vigil at the Shrine of Divine Love (October 12, 2013).

December 30: St. John Paul II, *Rosarium Virginis Mariae*, 15.

December 31: St. Alphonsus Liguori, *Hail Holy Queen*, 226.

Reflections

About the Author

Fr. Donald Calloway, MIC, a convert to Catholicism, is a member of the Congregation of the Marians Fathers of the Immaculate Conception. Before his conversion to Catholicism, he was a high school dropout who had been kicked out of a foreign country, institutionalized twice, and thrown in jail multiple times. After his radical conversion, he earned a B.A. in Philosophy and Theology from the Franciscan University of Steubenville, Ohio, M.Div. and S.T.B. degrees from the Dominican House of Studies in Washington, D.C., and an S.T.L. in Mariology from the International Marian Research Institute in Dayton, Ohio. In addition to *Under the Mantle: Marian Thoughts from a 21st Century Priest* (Marian Press, 2013), he has written *No Turning Back: A Witness to Mercy*, a bestseller that recounts his dramatic conversion story (Marian Press 2010). He also is the author of the book *Purest of All Lilies: The Virgin Mary in the Spirituality of St. Faustina* (Marian Press, 2008). He introduced and arranged *Marian Gems: Daily Wisdom on Our Lady* (Marian Press, 2014). Further, he has written many academic articles and is the editor of two books: *The Immaculate Conception in the Life of the Church* (Marian Press, 2004) and *The Virgin Mary and Theology of the Body* (Marian Press, 2005).

Fr. Calloway is the Vicar Provincial for the Mother of Mercy Province and the Vocation Director for the Marians.

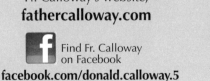

Marian Inspiration from Fr. Calloway

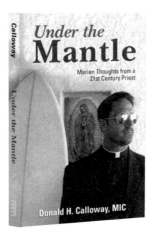

UNDER THE MANTLE: MARIAN THOUGHTS FROM A 21ST CENTURY PRIEST

Fr. Donald Calloway, MIC, deftly shares his personal insights on topics including the Eucharist, the papacy, the Church, confession, Divine Mercy, prayer, the cross, masculinity, and femininity. The Blessed Virgin Mary is the central thread weaving a tapestry throughout with quotes about Our Lady from Saints, Blesseds, and Popes.

UTM   9781596142732 *e*book: **EBUTM**

MARIAN GEMS DAILY WISDOM ON OUR LADY

In *Marian Gems: Daily Wisdom on Our Lady*, Fr. Donald Calloway, MIC, shares gems or quotes on Mary. He includes a gem for each day of the year, drawn from the writings of the Popes, Saints, Blesseds, and Venerables. When these gems first appeared in his book *Under the Mantle*, many readers loved them and suggested he publish them in a separate book for daily prayer. He was delighted and took their advice. Paperback; 232 pages.

MGEM   9781596143050

Marian Inspiration from Fr. Calloway

EXTREME MERCY II DVD

From run-away teen to Marian priest — Fr. Donald Calloway, MIC has inspired thousands of people around the world with his amazing conversion story. This new DVD combines Fr. Donald's incredible witness to God's mercy filmed live at the National Shrine of The Divine Mercy, with personal interviews in which he covers important aspects of his life and faith. 2 hours.

EXM2 9781596142886

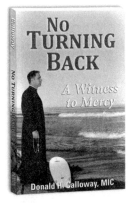

NO TURNING BACK: A WITNESS TO MERCY

In this bestselling book, Fr. Donald H. Calloway, MIC, shares his own dramatic conversion story, told with a compelling immediacy and honesty that will touch your heart. Popular Catholic author and apologist Peter Kreeft writes: "Read this book and watch the same wave lift Donald Calloway that lifted Paul and Augustine, Francis and Ignatius, from 'incorrigible' and 'impossible' to 'radically converted.' It's the old, old story, and it's irresistibly new every time. Here, it's told with winsome candor and simplicity by an ex-druggie, ex-criminal, surfer-priest." 262 pages, includes color photo section.

NTBBK   9781596142107
SPANISH: NTBBKS   9781596142282
Ebook: EBNTB

Marian Inspiration from Fr. Calloway

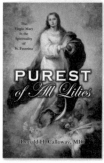

POAL
9781596141957

PUREST OF ALL LILIES: THE VIRGIN MARY IN THE SPIRITUALITY OF ST. FAUSTINA

This was the first book written completely by Fr. Donald. "It's basically my licentiate thesis on St. Faustina and the Virgin Mary," he explains. "It was edited to keep it from being too technical for a general audience." The book explores St. Faustina's rich relationship with the Mother of God, as recorded in the saint's *Diary*. Father Donald discusses the important lessons the Blessed Mother taught St. Faustina about suffering, purity of heart, and humility. He also includes an analysis of St. Faustina's poems that often use flower metaphors for Mary. 128 pages.

THE IMMACULATE CONCEPTION IN THE LIFE OF THE CHURCH

Paperback. 198 pages.
ICLC 9781932773934

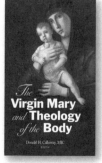

THE VIRGIN MARY AND THEOLOGY OF THE BODY

Paperback.
285 pages.
TVM
9781596141360

Call 1-800-462-7426 or visit fathercalloway.com

The Rosary is Mary's Prayer

THE HOLY ROSARY
You will treasure the meditations and colorful art accompanying every mystery of the Rosary in this booklet. Stephanie Wilcox-Hughes, 64 pages.
THRB
Spanish: THRS

PRAY THE ROSARY DAILY
Our most popular pamphlet includes Pope John Paul II's reflections on all four sets of mysteries of the Rosary. A complete guide to praying the Rosary.
PR2

MARIANS OF THE IMMACULATE CONCEPTION ROSARY GIFT SETS
These rosaries were designed exclusively for the Marians of the Immaculate Conception. They reflect our mission to spread the message of God's mercy through a devotion to Mary Immaculate. Each set comes enclosed in a matching gift box.
OMR3

Call 1-800-462-7426 or visit shopmercy.org

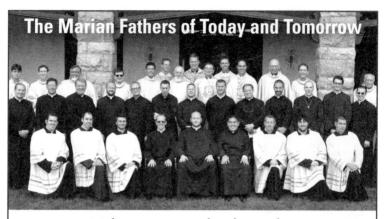

THIRTEENTH
OF THE MONTH CLUB

Fr. Donald Calloway, MIC,
Marian Vocation Director,
will participate in a recurring
feature in the Thirteenth of
the Month Club newsletter.

I'm honored and delighted to do this for the club, since it's a good way for me to help people come to a better place in their relationship with Our Lady. I want to let people know that by being in the Thirteenth of the Month Club, they're part of the Marian family. They are praying for us [the Marian Fathers of the Immaculate Conception], and we are praying for them.

Thirteenth of the Month Club members are a group of special friends who help support the work of the Marians of the Immaculate Conception. On the 13th of each month, members pray the Rosary for the intentions of the Club. The Marians residing in Fatima offer a special Mass on the 13th of the month for members' intentions. All members pledge a monthly gift and receive the Club newsletter published by the Association of Marian Helpers, Stockbridge, MA 01263.

For more information:
Call: 1-800-671-2020   Visit: marian.org/13th
Email: thirteenth@marian.org